Working for Spirit

Understanding the Way of Mediumship

Steven WK Scott

BALBOA.
PRESS
A DIVISION OF HAY HOUSE

Balboa Press books may be ordered through booksellers or by contacting:

Balboa Press
A Division of Hay House
1663 Liberty Drive
Bloomington, IN 47403
www.balboapress.com
1-(877) 407-4847

All cover images are reproduced courtesy of Tom Gibson Photography

Printed in the United States of America

ISBN: 978-1-4525-7708-1 (sc)

Balboa Press rev. date: 8/19/2013

Dedication
To Mum and Dad
- Together again

Table of Contents

Preface xi

The Legacy xv

Part 1: Understanding Mediumship 1

Chapter 1   You ARE Spirit 2

Chapter 2   Know Yourself 12

Chapter 3   The Mechanics of Mediumship 31

Chapter 4   Developing Mediumship 59

Part 2: Working for Spirit 67

Chapter 5   To be a Medium 68

Chapter 6   Finding your Spiritual Faith 93

Chapter 7   The Right Place 107

Chapter 8   Doubts and Trials 120

Part 3: Serving Spirit 133

Chapter 9   The Spiritual Connection 134

Chapter 10   Every Healing Thought 151

Chapter 11   Mediaship 165

Chapter 12   Positive Action for Progress 184

About the Author 191

Preface

ONE OF THE FIRST times that the Spirit in me became aware of its purpose occurred during a Sunday divine service at my local spiritualist church, in Ayrshire, Scotland. I looked up at the medium working on the platform and immediately felt an empathy to all that was taking place that evening. Not merely with respect to the role of the medium, but also with the process and act of communication with the realm of Spirit itself.

For a brief moment it felt as though the medium and I had traded places. There was a sensation of familiarity about the whole experience, a sense of belonging that I had not been prepared for. I knew that my own spiritual energy and hers could have easily traded places then and there. Deep down inside me there was something resonating with the event that echoed not necessarily with the act of Mediumship, but with the gift of communication and the importance of the truth of Spirit contact and the hope that it gave to this world.

I knew that this was not anything as simple as a desire or a need, but something else beyond that entirely. It felt almost like a calling. With hindsight I now know that it was Spirit just giving me a little nudge and a heads-up regarding the plans that were laid out before me.

Following the path of Mediumship was certainly something that I had never really thought of before in that way. I knew from working in development circles and from my growing up as a child that I had good empathy with others and could perceive some basic information from those around meat times such as feelings, emotions and intent. Yet, this was an entirely new experience and sensation.

I felt as though I was being made aware of a potential door opening in my future choices. Beyond that door lay a pathway so very different to the one I thought may have been laid out before me. All I had to do was to find the courage and resolve to step forward and acknowledge the very power that had opened it.

I knew that a personal journey into exploring the connection with Spirit lay beyond.

What I did not know, or could not see, at that time was just exactly the plans that Spirit, and thus my own Spirit, had laid out for me in this particular incarnation of life. I did not know, yet, what would be asked of me, or what I would ask of myself.

In that moment, all that mattered was that recognition of an affinity about the work that was taking place before my eyes which also applied to me. To be brutally honest about the experience I was not sure what to do with this realisation. In truth, the concept was actually both an intriguing, but also quite a frightening one.

As the years rolled by from that moment and my interest not only in Mediumship, but in the philosophy and teachings of Spiritualism grew, I never forgot that odd sensation.

As we are often wont to do at times I even fought against it, but it always seemed like the more I pulled away from Spiritualism and Mediumship, then the choices and events unfolding around me would always present that opportunity and requirement that I stay with the process. I know now that this was Spirits way of keeping my eyes focused on the road ahead, although some of the more severe and harsher lessons to do so I could easily have done without. Or perhaps not, for it was during the most difficult times that the Spiritual light grew in intensity.

Eventually, after much to-ing and fro-ing all it needed was that nudge from within me to make it happen. Like all great things, when the light of understanding fully same into focus, I realised that much of the hard work was already done in the years of toil and preparation leading up to this point.

When it came, it was like the flicking of a switch. All it took was for someone to breach that gap in my own belief in myself and to shine some perspective on my own self-worth. To give me the opportunity to believe in myself just helped to connect all the training and time spent in development together. In that moment, I realised that all this time it was the small voice inside of me that was doing the holding back.

I am so truly thankful to all those, in this life and in the Spirit realm, for giving me the strength, and belief in myself to accept and to be nudged. We are all truly possible of so much more than we often give ourselves credit for, and our Spirit is always so vividly aware of this.

We do not need to be fearless or bold. We do not have to be special or gifted.

All we need to do is listen to our heart and the miracle of our own worth unfolds, from within.

Steven Scott, November 2012.

The Legacy

WE ARE PART OF our own spiritual legacy, and all of us have amassed knowledge and carry experiences that stem from far beyond our mortal years. There is far more to our life and learning than just the brief moments of this particular period of existence than we could possibly know or imagine. Opening our eyes to our own legacy of Spirit is but one part of that process.

We are all part of one unified spiritual journey realised and nurtured by this universe in which we make our progress through our physical existence. Each and every one of us is on our own personal quest for some truth and understanding with regard to our purpose and role within all that we are and all that we may one day be.

We are driven to find and realise a meaning to our life, to discover the pathway upon which we may take those tentative steps toward personal growth and progress. This is not merely a physical desire but a part of who we truly are.

The need to know ourselves, to seek knowledge and purpose is not merely a part of our physical nature, but is a fundamental aspect to our true spiritual self. Our Spirit is not merely attached to us in this life, but is the eternal part of us that lives and learns beyond the transient nature of this physical presence. Our Spirit has chosen this life and this incarnation to once again be part of a physical realm and to experience all those moments of physical existence, for good or ill, in order that it may grow and learn.

In experiencing all that we can in this physical life, and by working and living through not only the positive but also the negative moments that we face, we nourish all aspects of our self.

Our challenge is to learn to recognise the essence of our true Spirit that lies within us at every moment and turn of the journey, for good or ill. To see beyond the mere physical life and to never let go of this connection to the spirit within, by finding the potential for growth during even the most difficult of circumstances is often the key to truly finding and connecting to our true, loving, spiritual self and nature.

As we are spiritual beings living a physical life, it is only natural that we can and do become easily become lost with regard to our true spirit and purpose within. In the need to preserve and protect the values we feel important to this physical existence, we often forget the light that we carry that is our true spiritual self.

Within these moments lie the greatest challenges for us to work with and overcome wherein the light of our Spirit truly begins to shine through and banish the darkness we create and the limits that we place upon ourselves.

This true spiritual light which is our true loving self cannot ever be extinguished, it cannot be tarnished, and it will always burn with a desire for understanding and learning. As each and every spirit within us rises to face the challenges placed before it, we are able to grow in so many wonderful ways.

Under a combined banner and purpose, so many have sought to establish and spread the word of a simple truth to the people of our world. Regardless of source or culture the message that our soul and spirit lasts eternal and that there is indeed more to our lives on this physical plane of existence, has always been in the consciousness of every living soul.

Spirit, and the methods and teachings of the messages of Spiritualism that have occurred throughout the ages, have always been around us. Those in Spirit have always sought to guide and direct us toward realising our potential with regard to the pursuit and understanding of our true spiritual selves. Always they have worked ceaselessly to promote the awakening of the spiritual legacy of each and every being.

Recorded throughout history are tales given by the wisest of sages from the very oldest of civilisations. Messages of hope and personal spiritual development have been passed to us from a variety of enlightened souls such as Silver Birch, Confucius, the Buddha and Jesus.

All these individuals have one unifying factor in their wisdom; each and every one opened themselves up completely to the divine source of all love and humanity.

Within the teachings and messages of philosophy and truth, they have always spoken not with regard to the deeds and accolades of physical world, but with regard to the nature of our spirit and soul that resides not externally but within our own eternal being. The words and wisdom taught to us identify that spiritual growth does not need religion and dogma but is about universal love of a divine nature and the connection that we share to that source.

In our own modern era, men of learning and philosophy, and the many pioneers of the modern Spiritualist Movement have sought to enlighten those around them. Like those teachers before them they offered us all guidance with regard to the true nature of our soul and the path that it wishes to follow as directed and guided by a divine purpose.

All these individuals and so many more have chosen not to shy away from the opportunity to unite with the divine within. They all acted to selflessly reach out to their brother and fellow man in an effort to heal and remove part of the suffering that is etched into our daily lives as we live this spiritual existence

Spiritual development, enlightenment and progress are not only open to a select or chosen few. We are all given the same opportunity to stop and take moments in life to reflect upon what is actually going on within our daily existence, and to recognise and remove the clouds and inhibitions that we place upon ourselves. We are always encouraged by spirit to look within and find the truth of the existence of our eternal soul, then to act in a way that is befitting a union with the divine source of love and spirit.

Within the understanding of our spiritual connection, the development of the process of communication has never been intended to cause hurt or harm or ill feelings by those who provide it. The messages have always been one of hope and continued existence beyond this life. They have been messages from one soul to another to encourage learning, trust and perhaps to remind us of our actual purpose in this place and time that we call our life.

Today, in this modern era, where the search for technology has overshadowed the understanding of the spiritual path laid out before us, the message was not delivered to a single soul but was given to many. All across the world our spiritual brethren reach out to us from Spirit with a simple message of for any who like those pioneers who have come before us, have the courage to step into this earth realm and live a physical life. This message is, like all great things, a very simple one, "Hello", "we are here", "we always have been here", "we are well and we love you, and it is time to move forward".

Historically, through the delivery of this simple message, open-minded men and women from all walks of life and levels of education have observed the evidence that the Spirit within is eternal and everlasting. These events made those that witnessed them not just believers, but which also served to remind them of the Spirit that they are, and so encouraged them in turn to become great advocates of the existence of Spiritual contact. This paved the way for others to stand up and take note of what was developing before their eyes. Even today we are still witnessing the development of human awareness of the realm of spirit, and the growing truth that existence beyond the end of our physical life is not merely a possibility, but an actuality.

Today, through the efforts of so many, Spiritualism and the evidence of our true Spiritual nature is now widely accepted as a modern science, philosophy and religion. We have the free will choice to investigate the Spiritual truth for ourselves, free from the limitations of human requirement and restrictive dogma. The all-encompassing wisdom of our own Spirit nature easily transcends these physical theories and boundaries to welcome all in its loving and boundless energy.

The pace and way of life between the past and the world today has changed dramatically. Even in the last twenty years we have travelled further along the technological route than in the previous one hundred and there appears to be no stopping the progress.

Yet, despite the momentum of human endeavour and accomplishment, is it possible that along the way we have somehow forgotten the very purpose of our existence in light of the methods of improving it in this physical world?

Is that simple messages of love and hope and spiritual truth that we received still required at all?

Where does our quest for the understanding and growth of our true Spirit nature belong in this world that we create for ourselves?

The truth is, with the dawning of the modern world and the changing social and political climates of recent years, from inhumane atrocities to global recession, there has never been a greater need for the world to stop and take a breath. We need to once again find the Spirit within and to seek our true spiritual purpose for living this life.

In your search for understanding and answers, look within and remember the past and all that you have conceived to get you to this point of your own journey. Strive to seek to understand the efforts and sacrifices of all those who have brought us to where we are today. Open your eyes to the light within and ask yourself if you, personally, are truly carrying the message that was first delivered "Hello", "we are here", "we always have been here", "we are well and we love you, and it is time to move forward". Then, trusting to spirit, dedicate yourself to the path you know is set before you.

It is your sworn birth-right promised by you, it is your true purpose behind your existence, and your Spiritual legacy to yourself. You only have to open your mind and heart to remember the truth.

PART I

Understanding Mediumship

Chapter 1

You ARE Spirit

Shaping our Spirit

WITHIN THE COURSE OF our human life we encounter a great deal of events that shape and change not only how we view our world, but also affect the manner in which we interact with it.

From our very first few independent breaths at birth until that moment when we pass beyond the physical extents of our life, all that we see and do is often defined and set out in physical terms.

The demands of this world, and the societies that we live in, require that we engage with the methods of progress, of conformity, of rationality and reasoning. They dictate that we comply with the laws, restrictions and regulations set down by those who have gone before us. In order to fit in and exist we must engage with the world around us, regardless of the role we ultimately must play.

There are some in this world who will be healers, and others who will become warriors or fighters; there are those who will effect great change and others who will bring setback and doubt.

As physical beings, living within a physical world we must fully interact with the changing environment and events around us on a moment by moment basis to ensure our continued existence.

As we grow, we are required to learn the ways and methods of survival in this physical existence, and as we learn we expand our knowledge and awareness we continue to change to meet the demands of the expanding world. In accepting a role in society we find our place to exist, and as we settle into our niche in life, our society and all the members within it continues to strive for existence not alone, but as a single entity composed of millions of individual parts.

This is a natural way of life for all who dare to enter into a physical existence and it is nothing to which we should feel ashamed of, or make apologies for. Yet, it is also vital that we learn to look beyond the mere physical aspects of our lives and take time to nurture and develop all aspects of our Self, not just the physical.

To imply or give priority only to our physical existence is almost to deny the fact that we are truly much more than just a mass of particles, chemicals and impulses that charge and fuel a biological system. We all have different and highly individual aspect of our personality and character that determines not only how we think, we laugh, we love, or we grieve, but which also serves to define the very nature of who we truly are within the physical limits of the body that serves us in this moment. We are able to contain and deal with the myriad emotions and passions that we possess, and to channel these sensations and impulses into very individual nuances of character, This allows us not only to define a sense of self, but also in turn to be defined with and to identify and connect to others. This then permits choice between similar individuals in whether or not they want to be part of our lives at any given time.

These are aspects of our character so vital to our development and progress that without them we would be little more than the most rudimentary of machines, living only to service our own needs and functions, and little else. Through our capacity to engage with thoughts, sensations, passions and expression of our own unique Spirit and personality, our character traits, flaws and foibles become a means of identification that applies only to our own self. Thus we begin to connect to the world around us in ways that differ from the merely mechanical and functional. We reach out, we make connections, we join together, and in doing so we achieve a sense of feeling for those around us through our empathy and understanding of what it must be like to be different, and in alternative circumstances to our own.

What is it then, beyond the mechanical and the chemical, that sets us apart from the rudimentary tools that we use on a daily basis within the modern world today? What is the fuel that ignites the sparks of individuality and expression in each of us? What aspect of ourselves can suddenly switch on to demand that we seek greater knowledge and understanding of not only who we are, but what we are?

The truth is very simple, so simple in fact that we often go out of our way to make it more than it actually is.

There lies at the very core of each and every one of us, a Spiritual identity that is our true, honest and genuine self. This spirit is uncluttered, pure, and resonates on a level with the energies of the world and the universe around it in a way that produces positivity, harmony and beauty in all that it touches.

Our true Spiritual self is not a destructive force, although it understands the need for removal and replacement of the unnecessary, but a force for advancement, for learning, and for attainment of knowledge and progress within positive means. It is the eternal and everlasting qualities we produce that identify us in our true light and which draw close around us those we love while we make our way through our earthly existence. It is the very fundamental core part of ourselves which is capable of producing true light, love and healing and which we have inherited from the divine source of all things. Specifically, the divine essence of the creative source of all that we see and experience, call it the Great Spirit, call it God, call it the spark of life, call it what you will.

Our Spirit cannot be taken away, it cannot be broken and it cannot be altered from its true positive source. These attributes are the purely physical aspects of ourselves that we apply to this life, on this level of existence. The physical, by its very nature, cannot impact upon our true eternal and spiritual self.

It is here, in living this physical life that we are affected by the physical demands and strains of the world around us. We try to gain and accumulate what we feel is important and to pull these things into our lives in order to justify our status or our place in the world around us. Yet, when we place alternate perspective on what matters to us, we often find that these things are relatively unimportant when taken into context with the examples of human loss and suffering that we see around us on a daily basis. Anyone who has lost a loved one to Spirit would readily understand that no amount of worldly goods can ever make up for the presence that is no longer there.

True Values

Our world has recently been hit with numerous natural disasters such as Tsunami and great tidal floods in New Orleans and Japan to storms of incredible magnitude raging across America and severe earthquakes in New Zealand and other countries. We have also recently seen rises in human conflict and wars, where many fight each other for territory or for the sheer sake of violence itself. Many thousands across the world have been forced to flee their homes, seeking shelter, asylum and aid in other places and countries.

Despite the damages inflicted by these events, and the sheer scale of the loss of physical items or possessions, many which lived through them, were overjoyed to simply have their loved ones safe by their side. Although the loss of physical things can and did have terrible impact upon the survivors, the emotions experienced do not compare to those who mourned the loss of their family and friends. That loss far eclipsed the destruction of the physical trappings that they had gathered around them.

As the world watched these events unfold over the past years, it emphasised and then acted. This action was to aid and assist, and to try and reduce or minimise in any way it can the trauma and emotion that was being experienced.

This is not the unreasoned response of simple biological machines devoid of feeling, but is the reaction of one Spirit, and one Soul responding to another in a desire to help, to heal, and to lessen the burden of life in any way it can do so. Why do we do this? We do so because we know the value of what is truly important, and we, who have been spared such trials, can truly understand the loss that has occurred. In each and every moment, our Spirit can feel and connect to the hurt around it, and can choose to respond.

This connection, empathy and compassion of the human condition will very often be the first and most direct contact we have with the true nature of our Spirit within. Often we do not need to be told whether or not an individual is hurt, in pain, or in need of even simple words of understanding in order to deal with issues that have become problematic for them in their life. The part of us that is Spirit can all too easily see beyond the veil and teachings of the physical world that we hide behind. The Spirit that you are instinctively recognises the Spirit within the person before us and resonates on a level beyond any physical need or requirement for words or clarity, for the language of Spirit is more than just explanation but one of understanding and awareness. It is instinctive and transcends the restrictions of our physical shell.

We must always be aware of and remember that we are not simply physical beings attempting to live a more spiritual life but that we are in fact spiritual entities who truly exist within a spiritual realm, that are living a temporary existence within a physical world.

To Spirit, this physical life is a place of learning, a place to adapt, grow and challenge ourselves. It is the place where we can realise the function of our true spiritual nature, despite all of the distractions, challenges and requirements that this world imposes upon us.

Our time here is fleeting at best when taken into comparison with our eternal soul and there is truly so much to do in that short space of time.

Before arriving on this earth plane you will have agreed on difficulties you will face this time around, have decided which the lessons you are to learn, you will have identified on how and who you will learn these with, and you will be looking forward to these experiences in a bid to grow and to understand yet more of the value of life.

Yet, when we begin and continue on our physical journey in this earthly realm the first and most difficult challenge is to retain that link to our Spirit within and to realise our learning potential. Only then can we begin to understand just how much of what we truly do is relevant to what we truly are and what we wish to become.

Our life in the physical world will demand that we give as much of ourselves as we can, that we focus on the demands that it places upon us and should we let it, time will pass and the fog of physical life will lift. Before we know what has occurred, our Spirit will once again be back home, but will we be able to say that we learned all that we came here to learn. Will we have remained aware of our Spiritual nature throughout and worked to the plan, or will we have become lost along the way, pausing only to check in to ourselves in a purely physical sense. I can imagine many who return back to Spirit and then think "Oh, I Knew I had something I was supposed to do down there!".

It is important that we connect fully not only with this life to make our progress, but also that we connect to our Spiritual nature.

When we stop to consider the events in our lives and the methods we used to make our way forward in the world, it does no harm to pause. To step back at times from the hustle and bustle of our daily existence and just take a few moments to meditate and listen to the voice within that emanates from the source inside of you.

Your Spirit will know what it truly wants and needs to grow, what it came here to accomplish, and how best to go about this. In contrast your physical self is locked into the patterns of this physical world and will assail you with logic and demands that require that you look at the world and where you are. If you let it, your physical self and ego will give you reasons to trust not in what you feel or acknowledge about your path in life, but to simply follow what has gone before. The physical self seeks only the physical needs for the extents of this life, the spiritual self is eternal and so will see the greater picture with regard to every individual's continuous development and so work toward that goal.

A Simple truth

These days I find myself consistently returning back to the simple source of truth that continually draws me toward the Spiritualist thought, faith, and philosophy. Everything comes down to recognition and understanding of the true Spirit within ourselves, and the universal connection to all things that we are intrinsically a part of.

We are not just with Spirit, and they are not just with us, but we ARE Spirit and OF Spirit. We are merely living what we know to be a physical existence at this time. The original aspect of us that represents whom we truly are, the part of us which is our higher self, has the capacity to exist externally from our physical body. It is the physical body that serves as a vessel for growth of the Spirit within. The physical is subject to the demands of life and the rigours of existence realised through emotional growth and physical change, but all of this serves to further teach and strengthen the true divine light within each and every one of us.

When we achieve this perspective we can see that everything we go through in this life is not simply a challenge to be endured, but another necessary experience that is fundamentally part of the key to our further spiritual development, provided we acknowledge and understand this.

In this life we are drawn to certain people and places, we develop attachments to friends, family, locations, animals and all those things that we feel we connect with. We form close bonds and associations not only on a personal or emotional level but also on a spiritual level as well. Perhaps those bonds were simply recognition of another Spirit or memory from another life that had once been shared, or perhaps they were new experiences or situations. In truth it does not matter, what is important is that the connections were made.

When eventually our physical existence ceases, the Spirit is again released to return back to the spiritual realm from whence it originated, however those bonds remain in existence simply because the spirit itself is eternal, it is the physical things of this world that are fragile and fleeting in their time permitted.

By making contact between our own unique Spirit and those around us, the true divine light and love that resides within the very core of us all meets with and recognises a fellow traveller and learner. This Spiritual light is untouched by the manifest problems and issues of this reality and existence, it does not care for the wants or worries of daily living, it is simply a purity that asks for nothing but appreciates everything. Yet it will always flourish and grow when its true nature is transferred from one soul to another, when that positive light is permitted to shine and the love that we all have contained within our Spirit is given the opportunity to touch the life of another.

Our spirit is eternal and those whom are no longer physically here with us in this life are never truly far from us for those loving bonds can never be broken. When Spirit communication occurs either personally or via a Medium, what takes place in that moment is recognition between one Spiritual being to another. As they reach out, they draw together the threads of spiritual connection that previously existed here in this life, and hen in doing so, touch that precious light within to give out healing, guidance and love when it is needed the most.

I have been fortunate to have met and spoken with so many people who have had to endure and work through so much pain, hardship, change and loss as well as all the Joy, Love and Fortune that has come their way through life. While many would have wished for things to have been or to have worked out differently, very few would ask that it all be taken back. Deep down we know and recognise that these were things we needed to go through in order to be who we are now. No-one ever said it would be a pleasant ride this time around but from the weakest and the frailest of individuals, I have seen the strongest and most determined of lights shine forth.

We are all born to be simultaneously warriors and ambassadors for spiritual growth in this life, changing as need be from time to time. Provided we never lose sight of the true nature of our own spiritual capacity, learning and understanding the need for everything we experience and acknowledging the power of the Spirit within, then we are always victorious over ourselves.

This is the challenge of our true spiritual self, to find our pathway in life by which we will live and learn and grow, then to translate and superimpose our full spiritual existence and journey into our physical lives. This is not an easy task by any means and requires that we not only understand the nature of our eternal Spirit, but that we look deeply into our own personal physical life, for how can we hope to distinguish between the two facets of our existence if we cannot truly say that we understand and know ourselves.

Chapter 2

KNOW YOURSELF

Recognise the True You

YOU ARE NO STRANGER to your Spirit, that pure and divinely inspired and loving part of yourself that is the real you. It is important that you first acknowledge and recognise this, for no-one can truly know the real you in any way, shape, or form, as much as the spiritual aspects and facets of your true self really does.

Always remember, you are a spiritual being that has chosen to be here, in this earth plane and place of mortal existence. You are here to learn and experience, to grow and remember what it is to be flawed.

You have chosen to challenge yourself to find, isolate and then try to overcome those flaws. You have chosen to make an effort to realise and recognise the moments when your true spiritual self is able to step forward and be felt, regardless of time, place or conditions.

At such moments your true loving light can and does shine and you know deep down that you have done something in tune with the true self. You will know that you have overcome all which has been hidden and buried beneath the mound of human woes, earthly restrictions and distractions that we heap upon ourselves in our everyday lives. You will know because you will see the benefit and impact that your positive actions have had not only on yourself but also on those around you.

This may well be something as simple as a basic act of kindness from one human being to another such as giving a shoulder to cry on or a simple offering of support. Alternatively it may be a more widespread act or actions of humanitarian relief. No one act is greater or more important than another, provided that they are all undertaken at a level equal to the capabilities of the individual at that time.

Someone who gives their last few coins to a homeless person or worthwhile cause is of equal, if not greater importance in the scale of things to the millionaire who presents thousands of pounds to a group of needy individuals. It is merely the scale of the giving and not the act in itself that changes. Those who do the best that they can with what they have are all working toward a greater place for all. Such people truly understand the difference that can be made with even the smallest of actions in relation to the impact on the outcome on humanity as a whole. If one individual act in one location can make a difference to the lives of one or more people, imagine the power for good that we could all accomplish in working together. All that stands in our way is the recognition of our capabilities and the limitations that we choose to place upon them, and the way we perceive them.

In recognising our current limitations and what we can both achieve and change, we have already taken the first few tentative steps toward reconnecting our spiritual self with the physical. We have begun the process of knowing our areas of what we can and cannot change in any one degree or aspect. Then, we can begin the process of moving forward slowly and continually expanding our influence over our limits until our goals are realised. Then, our Spirit shines and we begin to shape the world around us, all we need to do is believe in the power of Spirit within and all it can accomplish.

You Are Spirit. You must always remember that you are Spirit now, and always have been regardless of the human form you have chosen to take this time around in your search for learning and experience.

Shaping our Spirit

Within the course of our human life we encounter a great deal of events that shape and mould not only our perspective to and of the world, but also our place in it and how we should interact with the environment around us. These events and moments of guidance often come from those responsible for us and set in motion actions, thoughts and feelings that serve to set us on the paths for our future development. Yet how often does this actually meet the demands of the spirit within us in regard to achieving an understanding of the Spirits true purpose. How often are we merely facilitating a need for compliance with the structures of our own individual society?

I was blessed with wonderfully grateful parents, people who had tried for so long and were eventually not just happy but overjoyed to have a child in their lives. My parents did not care about the small eccentricities and foibles that showed up in my character from time to time, particularly those that were contrary to the common practices at the time. One time in particular that comes to mind was the manner in which, at an early age, I chose to write and use a pen or pencil.

I remember vividly in my childhood years, particularly primary school, where my teachers tried to stop me from something as simple as just picking up my writing implement in my left hand. They tried so hard to get me to change hands, using techniques that covered everything from telling me that it was 'bad' and an 'evil hand' to write with, through to cajoling me in front of the class for my lack of ability to write 'normally'.

Perhaps I had an inherited level of extreme obstinacy genetically passed down to me from my mother, for when she set her mind to something then nothing could sway her from it. Or perhaps it was my fathers' patience and sense of self and individuality that had somehow leaked its way down through the gene pool into my very bones that made me refuse to pick and write up with my right hand.

It may have come from some of the others in my environment for I even remember my grandmother telling me that 'no-one had the right to tell me what is the right thing to do, that knowledge can come only from yourself'. Perhaps, yet, it was a just a resonating aspect of my eternal soul from a previous existence in this physical world, resurfacing to reclaim a trait that it had always had.

Either way, I had the backing of a family of staunch self-aware individuals, and the presence of mind to realise that this was something that I had to do in this manner. Whatever the root causes there was clearly something that had rubbed off on this physical form and prevented me from taking up a right-handed writing approach to life.

To this day the attempts of my old teachers have never swayed me and I am still a devout left-handed writer, painter, thrower, pointer and thinker.

This is nothing special and does not hint or mean that I am in any way better or lesser than anyone else, for we are all born into this world having known our true and positive spiritual selves. We know deep down within our very souls exactly what we need to do in order to develop, learn and grow not just physically but spiritually within this life. The real test and trial for us, is to overcome those times when we simply choose not to acknowledge or listen to the voice inside. I retained my left-handedness simply because, no pun intended, it was right for me to do so.

Unfortunately, as we grow, the human part of us that we must see through the infant stage is in no fit state to do anything at all about out true nature. As we begin this life reliant on the support of other we must be nurtured to slowly adapt and develop as our body and awareness progresses and matures over time.

The task that we must overcome is to remain somehow linked with our spiritual self and as the human part develops, we find that link to our true self and tap into it. In addition, as self-aware individuals we also have a responsibility to ensure that our future generations are also made aware of their true nature. Beyond our own needs we must also to promote the truth of self-awareness to those who follow us.

Truly the manner in which we manage to find our spiritual self is unimportant in light of the actual happening and taking place of our own moments of self-awareness and understanding. This may occur at age six or sixty depending upon the circumstances that we set out for ourselves. The most important thing is that it does indeed happen, and that we recognise and acknowledge these moments with utmost clarity. In finding our true nature within these fleeting moments, we begin to know our true selves in this life.

A Voyage of Discovery

It can be very difficult to learn, or to recognise and know, your true self without first taking full account of the need for the physical nature of this existence. Our very existence is based on three aspects of our life. Our Body and our Mind have basic requirements for nourishment and stimulation that is based in a physical reality and without these needs being met, we struggle to function fully. Likewise, we live in a society that demands both understanding and compliance with accepted standards of action in order to function.

When we combine these physical factors of our life, it becomes apparent that we all need to eat, sleep, and find a place for ourselves in this world in order that we can progress our lives forward rather than stagnate in one place or condition. Given the importance of these very basic needs that our Body and Mind have, and often the difficulty that we experience in meeting these needs on a daily, weekly and yearly basis in the world today, is it any wonder that we often miss out on, or often neglect the third aspect of our selves, the Spirit.

So many of us work our way through this life less than whole, choosing to focus on the physical and mental trials and issues that raise themselves. This is not at all something that we should be either surprised with or anything that we should be ashamed of.

This is indeed a physical life and so the problems and issues that we find confronting us on a daily basis require that we focus ourselves upon them. It is no small wonder then that we all at times readily fall into the trap of allowing the physical existence to become dominant.

To make this even more difficult, this world is structured and has developed as such to imply that we are not only required, but expected to do all that we can to achieve and hoard more and more accolades, accomplishments, possessions and material gain. We are often measured by what we have accrued rather than what we are capable of and we pass this trait on from one generation to the next.

This easily gains momentum and demand until even the most fundamental of requirements becomes pushed far beyond the level of what was once deemed acceptable or exceptional. Is it any wonder therefore that we so easily lose our spiritual selves in the bid to keep up with the demands of the physical world in which we live?

To fully know ourselves however we must put into practice and learn to acknowledge and be mindful of all the aspects that we are created from. We must remember always that we are a human being with unified need for nourishment of Spirit, Mind and Body combined. It is not enough to simply pursue the few parts of the path which appeal to us throughout our lives. If they do, then while we live on, neglecting the unity of all aspects, there will ultimately come a time when we become reliant on the part of our nature that we have neglected for too long.

In such circumstances then we come across moments of difficulty and crisis in ourselves, primarily because the path we have taken is not in accordance with our true needs and requirements. Deep down we are all too aware of this. Deep down, we even fear this challenge to our beliefs and to our standards.

Can we truly say that this is in keeping with our Spirit within? Can this truly be what our Spirit needs? How well do we know our Spirit at all?

Spiritual Cognizance

In choosing to know one's own Spirit, we are required to be completely and totally honest with all that we have so far achieved to date. This will demand that we draw upon all our reserves, asking that we go deep within and uncover a great deal of personal courage and determination as we will be required to focus choices that we have made which we may not want to look too deeply into.

This includes both the good and the bad, both of which we will be required to make peace with before we progress. Through this we will eventually begin the task of reflection and understanding of our most fundamental needs and what it means to have these realised or denied. In doing so, we learn to acknowledge the reasons behind why we succeed or why we fail and so learn to develop compassion, empathy, and well-being for not only those around us, but also for our own self. For how can we understand and forgive others, when we all are so intent of carrying our own baggage and demons around for the rest of our days. Remember, this is also our journey, and we must be as ready to forgive ourselves as we are ready to forgive others in order to allow healing and progress to take place.

This journey will demand great bravery and genuine intentions in line with our true spiritual learning process in order that we may accurately see just who we are, where we are going, and what we must do to get there.

When we manage to accomplish this, all of a sudden our vision can become clear and the answers to our problems appear before us, then we must choose to act upon them or not.

At such times of clarity and understanding, the world and all those around us in both the physical and the spiritual realms will be in alignment with our own needs and when we do take these steps toward positive change and growth, everything will become easier. Actions will bear positive fruit and we will feel at peace with the situation, for we will be at peace.

This state will occur and feel natural because we have chosen what is best for us and what permits us to grow and challenge ourselves.

We may not be at first comfortable with our choice to follow the spiritual path, because we know that we are being challenged by ourselves in the most personal sense. But deep down we know that we can often be our harshest yet also our most forgiving judge if we are only able to forgive ourselves.

There is no easy route to knowing and recognising what you truly are and what you truly need, and there are no quick fix methods for improving. We now life in a highly technological age where many of our problems can be side-lined for a brief period or where we can permit distractions to take over and lead us away from the issues at hand.

In truth the greatest risk to our development is our own sense of need for results and the worst blind alley we can chase our progress down is invariably the one which leads to the most immediate source of gratification. Unlike machines we cannot simply exchange a few chips or throw in a new data card to be upgraded with more physical gain or spiritual harmony.

When we want to improve we must embrace all that comes with this decision and engage fully and completely with the process. This requires constant work and continual assessment of the direction and purpose behind our actions in this physical existence as well as monitoring of how much we have come to learn not only about our subject matter, but about ourselves and how we deal with everything this path we have chosen has to offer.

We must connect with the very core of our being, recognise the needs of our combined Mind, Body and Spirit, and then find and nurture our every aspect of our self.

Find Yourself

How do we do this?

Having spent a great deal of our lives both living and making our way through this physical existence, it must seem like a very difficult task, and if you focus only upon all the external influences and factors affecting us every day, it can be.

Like many of the most powerful methods of self-realisation, the concept of finding oneself is invariably a very simple one that we make very difficult to undertake indeed. We must learn to let go of everything excess that no longer serves us, and to strip away all the roles and facades that we create and present to the world. In honestly and completely choosing to let go of all that we do not need, what is left behind is therefore everything that serves us better.

This is no small or easy task, but how can we hope to look honestly at our self when we are hiding behind so many false fronts that we barely even recognise our own needs. By releasing all that is no longer of use, we can begin to get our first glimpse of who we are and what we truly need and therefore begin a process of not just self-realisation, but also self-healing as a great deal of what we carry in our hearts and minds can and often does tie us in to past events, particularly those issues and events that hurt of affected us emotionally in some way.

Often, many of the issues that we carry are not even our own, but those of others whom we have come into contact with. How often have we been hurt or badly affected by the words of others, and every time we revisit or remember them the emotion all comes rushing back.

Train yourself to release and let go of all negative thoughts and feelings, use visualisations, meditations, writing, whatever exercises work for you to release and let go of all negativity and then make peace with the event as best you can. This is a lifelong goal, for we cannot go through our lives without meeting some form of conflict. Release, forgive, let go.

Letting go of the past in order to clear up and remove the excess from within ones perspective is part of this process. Then, making use of this renewed vantage point to re-assess and move forward can be, and again often is only the first step in the process of getting to know ones true self.

We must learn to evaluate not only our self but also our strengths and weaknesses, our thoughts and actions, our beliefs and our prejudices, our wants and our needs, and all other facets of our character inside and out, upside and down, backwards and forwards. As always we must begin this task by focusing in upon ourselves, for this body and this existence is the vessel in which everything rests and resides and nothing is going to change it other than the thoughts, feelings and actions that we choose to undertake.

It is vital that you learn to know yourself and work with everything that you have, for good or ill. Remember there is nothing wrong with wanting to change and develop either personally or spiritually, however you must be realistic and understand the scope of what you are able to change. Your ego will demand instant results but your spirit will know that these take time to develop, for the greater time you spend cultivating and nourishing the soil of your soul, the stronger the fruits of your labours will be.

There are many means and methods of self-development available today, each one as varied and alternate as there are individual needs within each one of us. Find the methods that work best for you, this may take months or even years in order to do so, and you may change both disciplines and direction more than once in order to achieve your goal of knowing yourself. Be honest and do not look for the shortcuts, deep down you will know what is working and what you need to do.

Maintaining Momentum

There may be times when you falter along the way, when you will stumble and lose track of your goals and where you will become wound up once again that physical life that demands so much form and function from all of us. This is fine, for these are not failures of your journey at all but can often be necessary rest periods you are required to take. Perhaps, at such times what you need most of all is to stop pushing and to pause, maintain, tread water, and restore the balance of power within your being once again.

Remember that you are never alone; all those around you in spirit are watching carefully and will give you all the assistance they can at every opportunity, all you have to do is just be open, receptive and aware of what they say and when they say it.

I recall working on a charity evening one day and the wonderful and gentle soul of a lady stepped forward to with a message for one of the congregation. She came through clearly and identified herself and the daughter that she was looking for. It was up until then one of the most accurate messages I have ever experienced. Everything about her was gentle and quiet and peaceful until she gave me the most harsh and rebuking message to deliver, nothing nasty or vulgar or offensive but very stern indeed. Naturally, being caught on the spot at the sudden change in this Spirits demeanour, I was off well off balance and had to inform the lady in the audience that her lovely mother was more than a little irate. Choosing my words carefully I relayed the message only to be rebuked once again by the lady from Spirit.

"Tell her exactly the way I told you" this Spirit said to me. I apologised to the lady, indicated that her mother had just given ME a telling off and relayed the message to her.

"You are trying to do too much, too quick, all at once, you never listen and you are getting nowhere at all. You need to crawl before you walk" her mother asked me to relay. I had no idea at all what she was talking about as she never said, but I could see tears well up in the eyes of her daughter so she clearly knew exactly what it was in relation to.

At the end of the evening, this lady approached me and said "Son, I didn't think you were giving the message to the right person, until my mum made you give me into trouble. It was exactly the way she used to say things and it felt as though she just jumped right out of you at me. It was exactly what I needed to hear"

I am very confident that she listened and took on board her mothers' words. I certainly did not have a choice, so strongly did her mother want to get the message through to this lady that her Spirit saw fit to give both of us a little positive, corrective action that evening.

I learned to trust that Spirit knows exactly what to say to get the point across, and that they are always vigilant when it comes to the lives of their loved ones in this earthly existence. They want us to progress; they want us to improve and the do so want us to rediscover our true spiritual nature and to make this manifest positivity in the world.

Stay Grounded

It is vital that we remain grounded and focused as we progress along our own individual spiritual journey. We often set out with the greatest of intentions, to serve and to be of service to the divine source and all its manifestations and to be able to reach out and help those who need it most.

Yet it is all too easy to become caught up in the desire or rewards we receive during the quest. Often the most purely intended words of praise or thanks can lead us into patterns of self-delusion or denial if we let our Ego be involved. Instead always be true to your Spirit and remain mindful of the purpose of helping others, to ease suffering and pain they experience in their lives. When you accomplish and succeed, let it go and allow your Spirit to be free of it in order to remain focused on the next task at hand.

It can also be so easy to lose track of ones' purpose amid the drive to improve and build upon our experiences and development. At such times we can often lose sight of the reasons why we are choosing to walk this particular path, leading us to choosing wrong decisions along the way that ultimately hinder our spiritual growth and undermine the actions we are trying to achieve.

As mentioned at the start of this chapter we must always remember that we are spiritual being living a physical life, not physical beings attempting to be spiritual.

True spiritual work is done with a genuine divine purpose and one which stems from progression and promotion of the divine love and healing that is the birth right of us all to achieve. Yes this is a physical world, and we need the physical means and measure to survive in it, but we should never lose sight that we are merely the physical instruments of a greater power. We are only the conduit and not the generator and we must be respectful of the power and privilege that has been presented to us by being given the opportunity to work for the realm of Spirit and the divine source of life.

You will know when you work in the power of positivity and purity that resonates with your true spiritual being. For all you do will be part of the very power from both Spirit and the Divine. All your actions will feel right to your Spirit and Soul in every aspect and fibre of your being. You are and always will be the very best judge of the honesty of your purpose in Service. Yet you must listen to the Spirit within in order to know.

In addition to our own Spiritual awareness, and of equal importance, is the need to remain grounded and focused upon the nature of Service and the task at hand.

Whether you are a Medium, a Healer, a Reiki practitioner, an Angel worker or any other type of spiritual specialist, every spiritual discipline has its own unique methods and means of being put into practice. All require that you also work consistently to leave behind all the excess baggage that you accrue throughout your life, and simply ask that you do not become obsessed with the building of spiritual accolades, complements, accomplishments or benefits.

Naturally we must all work hard and consistently, this gives us more knowledge of our chosen fields, more refining of our ability and increases our own personal 'toolkit' of workable skills. Yet we must also remember that we do not need to be able to do everything, sometimes, often-times, we are better placed to serve by focusing upon only a few specific skills as opposed to harbouring numerous outlets for development. Remember the saying "Jack of all trades, but master of none".

Yes, we need to experiment and test our boundaries and push our limits in order to better serve both Spirit and the divine, but then we must also learn to let go and release all that no longer serves you, particularly when our reasons for holding on to it are not of a Spiritual, but a purely Physical nature.

Holding onto and relying upon many of the practices we encounter, and there are thousands if we open ourselves up to everything, is a manifestation of our Ego and that need to build and hoard and find reason and cause for difficulties. It is, in effect, the opposite direction from that in which that we need to be progressing.

Working with Spirit is essentially a very simple process and ultimately does not need rituals, crystals, mantras, cards, foci or anything else. It is the human, doubting part of ourselves, fuelled by the ego that puts the doubts and dependency upon us that these are requirements. Essentially all that is required is the Spirit in front of you, the Spirit inside you and the Spirit who wishes to communicate. When we learn to abandon the physical restrictions and doubts that we will inevitably put upon ourselves then our spiritual light glows strong and clear, and the communication become so much easier to establish, for it is purer and less burdened by this world and the restrictions we place in it.

It is in our human nature to try and restrict our development and to look for the reason to abandon what we may wish to pursue and too often not do things. Many of us struggle to focus on and control the negative thoughts of our ego with regard to their physical life never mind being able to consider even looking into a spiritual life.

This is not wrong and again is not in any way a failure on our part, it is simply where we are within our own individual journey and does not mean to say that with the right time and guidance, we cannot begin to overcome the difficulties that life has put in front of us and begin to make progress for ourselves.

Coping with Difficulty

Even when we encounter the most difficult times of trial in this life, there is often a greater meaning to be realised and understood behind all the pain and suffering that we may be feeling. We simply need to quiet down the mind and body and find that connection to the Spirit within and the divine guiding light that we all ultimately link to and remember that, regardless of the position we find ourselves in, that this learning experience is what we have come here for, that this situation is the reason for our earthly existence, and that we are strong and in facing what we fear we become that much more capable in every aspect of our lives.

In Spiritualism, we understand that we have chosen to experience key challenges throughout our lives in order that we can further our understanding of our life and so grow that little more with every gain and loss that we encounter.

The more I experience the extents and limitation presented to me within my own life, the more I realise that the majority of who and what we are as human beings is determined not by how we easily make our way through the challenges we face, but what we learn from overcoming them.

Every time a situation arises that pushes my boundaries, I know that am required to stop, take note and reassess sometimes not only who and what I am, but also where I feel comfortable 'being' and 'living' with regard to the choices that I have made. I then need to respond to this and choose how I will move beyond this particular point in life, physically, mentally, or spiritually.

There are many of us in this world who choose to 'exist', and not to 'live' to the full extent of our potential. These individuals can, and often do, appear to be like lost or confused revenants of human frailty who amble through their lives in a state of disconnection. For many reasons they become lost along their path and often they are unaware of the beauty and diversity around them. Even with the help and aid of others only they can choose whether or not to remain blinkered to the scope of the human spirit and all it can attain and impact upon.

We must always remember that all of these individuals are no different to anyone else. More likely than not they have chosen to experience a life that requires them to face challenges that most of us could not hope to understand or weather. Learning does not always come from the wonderful and the positive, very often the harshest situations can bring about the greatest seeds of understanding.

Yet others have set their path upon this world with the purest of intentions in their choices, but have not yet risen to the challenges presented before them and have chosen to become a sleepwalker within their own living dream that has become their existence. In some respects these people become literally nothing more than purely grounded physical beings that continually ostracise themselves from the real spiritual truth that is their natural inheritance to themselves. Moreover their physical demands and desires sometimes do little more than spiral into punishing themselves for tasks not yet done or fulfilled. It is easy to lose ones way on any spiritual journey.

In order to find ourselves, to realise our true purpose, we have to choose to take the first few tentative steps along the route toward our spiritual awakening. This is never easy but we must always remember that we have come here in the sure and certain knowledge that we have chosen to walk this spiritual path that lies before us.

No-one, particularly ourselves, said this would ever be easy or pleasant but the rewards and benefits of finding strength in adversity, belief in times of tragedy, and hope in the darkest of moments can far outweigh all that we experience in every inch gained throughout our trials.

In choosing to advance, we are accepting responsibility for ourselves and for what we need to learn in this life we lead, not just for ourselves but often for the benefit of those with whom we both rely upon and aid every day of our lives.

Be of Service

In remaining focused on service, and ensuring that when we work we choose to do so within our power to positively change what we can, in small ways, to benefit everyone around us every day of our lives, then we are truly are choosing to live spiritually within ourselves.

In working to be the best that we can we are automatically becoming more spiritually aware of our trials and shortfalls with regard to how we deal with the world around us. We can therefore recognise the issues and problems of others and it becomes easier to just forgive and let go of any attachments that we have which may keep us from moving onward and progressing not only in our human existence, but in our spiritual one as well.

For those who seek to develop that link to Spirit, it is essential that they first take the time and effort to get to know themselves in all aspects of their life both in a physical and in a spiritual sense before they even begin to know how to connect back to that realm of spirit from which we originated.

It takes time, effort and patience to work with oneself and to understand not only our needs and desires, but to see where our spiritual pathway is leading. Remember that we are not only the ones on the journey, but also the makers and directors of this path to begin with. There is no rush for we do know what we have to do in order to progress, all we need to do is lose everything else that clutters the way forward and no longer serves us faithfully.

Only when we have aligned our intent in the here and now with the intent that we put in place before this physical life can we hope to find our route forward. By taking the first few tentative steps toward knowing and finding our spiritual self, we can finally illuminate our path.

Take your time, and savour the journey.

Chapter 3

THE MECHANICS OF MEDIUMSHIP

We can all develop

I PREFER TO AVOID using the term 'Gifts' whenever it comes to speaking about Psychic, Mediumistic or any other form of Spiritual awareness and discipline. Making use of the term 'Gift' can and often does give a false sense of impression that these abilities have been bestowed upon only a select few chosen to receive them. Nothing could really be further from the truth.

The only real 'gift' involved is that which we all possess, a divine connection through our true spiritual self to the source of light and love that has been made available for all of us, here in this life, to do with as we choose. It is through this connection that we recognise our divine nature and the capacity that we possess to connect to the world around us.

Each and every one of us possesses the power and capability to develop both our inherent psychic skills and to further our mediumistic abilities to some degree or another. We are capable of honing and developing upon the current level of awareness we have to the best of our abilities, and we always have the option of seeking continual improvement of these abilities throughout our lives and beyond.

There are no hard and fast rules for this and the path to

development is as unique and individual as we are from one another. Yet, despite all our differences in character and personality, we are all connected by the spirit within us and so possess varying levels of skill and capacity for improvement. What we must remember is that all we aspire to become is dependent upon our personal nature, our lifetime of related spiritual experiences, and our personal psychological make-up and system of beliefs that we choose to invest in and it is there that we often place barriers or blocks in the way of our spirituality and capacity for learning and developing.

In respect to this, given that we live a rather diminished and inhibited version of our true spiritual capacity in this earthly life, being aware of our capacity to choose and alter the course of our journey is a necessary requisite to any progression.

One of the most influential barriers to this is often the fact that we are subject to the pressures and emotions of this life and existence. It is our own personal responsibility to remind ourselves of just what it is that we are trying to work with, and to accomplish, when we work with and tune into our psychic faculties.

Before we do so, though, we must always be able to find a place to begin our journey of improvement that is clear of both desire and purpose. It is never enough to simply want to develop ourselves for our own sense of self-worth and need. Our spirit, and indeed the world of Spirit, deserves so much more than this. To treat your development as nothing less than the vehicle of earthly requirement and fulfilment, such as becoming well-known or famous, or as a means of power and control over others is to treat not only the service you provide with disrespect, but also ensures that whenever you work, your motives are not necessarily in the correct place to function as they should.

Spirit does recognise that it requires a great deal of work and development in order to do your best and they will ensure that you never lose out or are adversely affected. However, we must be prepared to listen to the spirit within and to act accordingly with the purpose and meaning of what it truly means to be a medium and to work for others.

Before we can ever hope to work with Spirit, or even to start working with our own Psychic faculties, we must first come to terms with and understand the nature and function of the energy systems we are attempting to integrate with. Regardless of whether we are undertaking either psychic or mediumistic communication, for how can you hope to accurately work with any knowledge or power if you do not yet know what it is that generates and facilitates the very energy you are working with.

It is never enough to just sit and hope that the information will come to you. Like all natural processes and systems of energy there must be first a basic understanding of how it works before you can begin to recognise and control it.

Before we can learn to control any source of external factors, it becomes vitally important it is that we consistently expand not only our awareness, but also our knowledge of our self before we embark on any form of development. External control can never be put in place of our own internal controls have been neglected or ignored for any period of time. If we cannot control ourselves, what chance to we have of exerting control on the world around us?

The very basics of Psychic and Mediumistic

The only real place to begin is with oneself. Begin by working toward achieving at least a basic foundation and level of awareness of the person that you are, what motivates you, what makes you want to do this, what purpose will this serve you and others? Be warned, this is an on-going process and rarely if ever comes to us easily but does require the greatest amount of honesty with yourself. It may take ten days or it may take ten years before you are comfortable looking at the person you are and knowing your methods and reasons for wanting to develop. Regardless of the time, be honest and truthful.

Then, when you have some clarity of mind with regard to yourself and the nature of your reasons for wanting to development, you may want to personally start investigating and experiencing the difference between what is Psychic work and what is Mediumistic work. Both of these energies are often so closely linked that from time to time and it can be easy to fall out of one and into another, particularly during mediumistic links with Spirit.

To help explain this connection, and the difference in nature between them, I have used the terms 'Communicator' to identify the source of the information received, 'Recipient' to identify the sitter or person intended for the message, and 'Medium' or 'Psychic' to identify the means by which the communication is channelled.

Within a Psychic connection, the recipient is often also the facilitator of the Psychic communication themselves, while the psychic taps into and 'download' the information psychically from the recipient to be relayed back to them. This process is extremely different from that undertaken to create a mediumistic link and utilises a personal energy exchange between all those present in order to achieve communication or information. There is generally no outside or third party energy involved unless more two or more psychic or recipient sources are present.

Within a Mediumistic connection, the communication is three-way and will be referring to the Spirit Communicator who will approach the Medium direct and speak to them to relay the information to the recipient.

The energies utilised by both the communicator and the recipient during Mediumistic connections are always affected by the very mechanics required to make the process work. Without understanding the mechanics, there can be no good and reliable means of actual communication. Yet, before we begin to work on our capacity to achieve a mediumistic connection, we must first be able to control and make use of our own psychic capabilities.

Although both methods can work together to produce successfully accurate information depending upon the circumstance and the type of reading or connection that is being made, they are invariably very different methods of communication. However both disciplines in fact make use of similar but equally different skills and methods of approach.

Defining the Psychic

'Psychic' is a term used to define the development and use of skills which, as the name suggests, are purely psychic in nature and do not necessarily rely on any source out-with that of another physical being or object in order for the effect to take place.

We all have a psychic aura and field that surrounds us and this aura is subject to change depending upon our moods, emotions, stresses, reactions or lack thereof. The field is both expandable and retractable and can extend easily out and away from the body, particularly when we focus upon a specific task with regard to extending our awareness through this auric field.

If you have ever walked into a room and just 'felt' that there was something odd with the place at that time, this could be due to an extension of your psychic awareness and aura with an empathic residue within the room. You pick up on the emotions and feelings that were there before you arrived and your own psychic awareness reacts to this, often presenting you with a small sensation or feeling that may have been attributed to the events that took place there.

Emotions are perhaps the simplest and most easily transferred emanations that may be picked up on psychically; I remember as a young boy often coming home from school and as soon as I reached the front door I could tell straight away when things were not quite right at home. Perhaps my parents had had an argument, or some bad news, or there was another person in the house whose own aura was different from my parents. Whenever it happened it felt like a palpable change in the whole environment, rather like walking into a bubble of thicker air, which I never truly understood until much later in life for what it truly was.

My own psychic aura and awareness was so attuned to the normal running of the home in which I lived that I could easily pick up any change in the environment. Yet again I must stress that there was nothing in any way 'Gifted', unusual or 'supernatural' about this. If anything it was entirely natural and simply the result of an open and receptive mind on the world and the energies within it.

This is an example of the skills that we all possess and all can work with and is often the very simplest stage of development that we can all undergo as part of our training or perhaps even our daily existence. Emotions and feelings are often the most pure, unrefined and unfiltered of reactions and as such they are often 'out there' and in our aura even before the body has reacted by changing expressions or mannerisms.

Just listen to the sound of someone who is losing their temper, you can almost feel the change occurring around them before any alteration in the tone of their voice and far in front of when you actually experience it happening.

This is not necessarily limited to people, for places also carry their own psychic residue that we can tap into., There are times where you receive both visual and psychic clues about locations without the need to venture far into them. You only need to look down a darkened alley to logically know that it is unsafe, but if you take a moment to open yourself up you may feel and experience the sensations of warning, potential danger or general discomfort that are our primal urges to seek out a safer route.

These are not just learned responses but are also our aspects of our psychic self-defence mechanisms kicking in to protect us. It does no harm to listen to these and we should not let the ego over-ride them, we developed these for a good reason.

Our basic psychic skills such as emotional empathy, area awareness and danger senses are very simple psychic faculties that we all possess. As with all psychic abilities, they work primarily from within ourselves and then focus outward and are dependent mostly upon the psychic aura and faculties that we all possess to one degree or another. For some it is done personally and for others a focus or system of directed thought is used, such as tarot cards, a crystal foci, or even charms and rituals etc. Although the methods change, the underlying energy utilised and worked with is ultimately the same in all Psychic connections.

Many psychic skills are information gathering and communication tools such as: Empathy: or the sensing of others emotions; Telepathy: the reading of another thoughts; Psychometry: the reading of objects for information; and Remote Sensing: the viewing of faraway locations, people or places; to name but a few. There are other psychic abilities which have a more physical component to their application such as: Psychokinesis or the movement and manipulation of objects, or Psychic Surgery and Psychic Healing, where the focus is on aiding and curing individuals or oneself.

When anyone works psychically they are the ones who power their own particular individual psychic abilities and capability from within their own psychic aura and self, before they finally manifested and project it outward to create a specific effect. There is no other party required to be involved in the event other than the one creating the effect, and the recipient of the particular psychic event.

Very often, as in the case of information gathering abilities, the recipient is often the same person as the one who creates the effect in the first place. Perhaps this is why so many cases of psychic awareness are often more accurate on a personal level than those which require contact with a third party or external source.

During the psychic connection you will be tuned in primarily to the recipient and will feel that connection very strongly as images and events from their life pass between the connection in their auric field to yours and vice-versa. There will be an almost palpable and definite bond between both of you as you link in to their energy and it will feel like you are reading or downloading the information directly from the source itself. If a psychic were using tools or others items, like cards, pendulums, rituals etc., these would serve to focus and strengthen the link even more as both communicator and recipient are actively participating in the task. This can and very often does give stronger and more defined information that links to their past, present and future courses, such as you would receive in a good Tarot Card reading.

In short, the Psychic is the one who powers and communicates the findings of their own their own ability and then delivers the results received or created directly back to the individual recipient concerned.

Defining the Mediumistic

Mediumship, due to the nature of how the bond between the communicator and the recipient is established, feels very different to a purely psychic link. The ebb and flow of energy does not take place primarily between the Medium and the recipient, but between the Medium and the Spirit Communicator. As such the energy involved is spiritually lighter in sensation, not being so grounded and concerned with the physical moment. The connection glides easily between the Medium and the Spirit communicator, perhaps due to the energetic exchange being less focused on result and more focused on flow and maintaining the connectivity. In effect the medium becomes both the primary receiver and secondary communicator in a very active way.

The Medium must question and seek the information, rather than sit back and enter into the psychic field of the recipient and wait for what they are to be given. The actual intended recipient of the message is the secondary, yet ultimate, receiver of the message itself. It is to them that the medium channels the messages toward, and it is Spirit who picks up on and recognises the responses themselves, not the medium who relays it back. The medium is merely the conduit for the connection from spirit to this earthly realm. Spirit is aware of all we do and does not necessarily require that the medium give the response back to them, after all, they are there and watching their loved on as they receive the message.

This pattern and flow continues until the full message is delivered and, as you can imagine, requires that the medium make use not only of the Spiritually developed faculties of mediumship and communication, but also their own personal awareness and

Psychic abilities of their connection to the recipient and the Spirit entity at all times during the communicative process.

While all mediums are in some way psychic, not all psychics are mediums. The use of psychic abilities does not in any way imply that an individual has mediumistic ability.

Many psychic abilities are innate and specific to an individual, requiring that we seek to improve them rather than have to learn them.

Mediumistic ability however requires to be learned to some degree over and above this natural psychic ability that we all have. The basic requirements of communication between a medium and Spirit communicator always requires some continuous development of psychic faculties in order to work effectively on all levels and receive the communication as it is being delivered. However, all the information being provided to the medium that forms the basis of the message to be delivered comes solely from an outside third-party source, being that of the Spirit communicator themselves, and not from within the medium or being picked up from the recipient.

As a result the 'feel' and energetic link between a Spirit communicator via a medium to a Recipient feels vastly different to that type if energy utilised and established during a purely psychic communication, or sensing from within one's own self, to that of a recipient.

During the mediumistic communication, the medium is merely a conduit between the Spirit and the person for whom the message is to be received. This link is not directed outward toward the recipient but outward toward the communicator with a focus of remaining aware of the recipient. Essentially, if this were a telephone line direct to our loved ones then they would be the start-point telephone, the recipient would be the end-point telephone and the medium is the miles of cable or radio waves between the two.

Why and How does Spirit Communicate?

During a mediumistic communication, the contact in spirit will be working directly to relay whatever information they can to you. This is in order to identify themselves and be made known to the recipient so that they are both recognised and understood to be the giver of the message.

Often the spirit contact will work to give evidence of their character, their life and their connection to the recipient and will wish to make them aware of their presence and aid before giving some words of hope, consolation or assistance to guide them through events in their life. To do this, the contact will be continually working through all the mediums senses, using whatever means they can to get the message through.

During any one contact, your friend in Spirit may well make use of: Clairsentience, the transmitting of sensations and feelings; Clairaudience, the transmission of sounds, words or even whole sentences; Clairvoyance, the transmission of images, shapes or pictures; or even Clairalience and Clairgustance, the transmission of smells and tastes. This is where the mediums own psychic faculties come in and where Spirit will work with the best possible and most developed link within each medium to ensure that as much information as possible is relayed.

As each medium will have different strengths and weaknesses within their psychic faculties, so too does the information brought forward change. Some mediums have great Clairaudience, while others only hear certain sounds; some can vividly describe persons and places, while others receive only colours; perhaps they can feel and sense what the Spirit contact wishes to portray but hear and see nothing at all. The communication is also dependent upon what method the Spirit contact is also trying to portray. A spirit who spoke little in this life is likely to do the same when they come through because this is fundamental to them being recognised and their character trait being brought forward. Truly the list of possible combinations and means of communication can be endless.

The mediums job is to try and process, organise and then try to relate all of the information they receive and then give this over to the recipient. This is no mean task, for often the spirit contact is so very overjoyed to be given a change to once again speak and relate evidential information and memories to the recipient that very often the flow of information is excessive or fragmented by the time the brain and faculties of the medium catch up. However, regardless of evidence and outcome of any message, there is always sensations and emotions of love, support and a desire to help us in our daily endeavours and trials from all those who do work so hard to communicate from the realm of spirit to all of us here on this earth plane.

An Active Process

Being a Medium does not simply require that we offer up our services to Spirit, and they will answer in a clear, concise and easily identifiable way. The truth is actually far from this.

In attempting to make our connection to Spirit, the medium must be an active participant in the process and must consistently work to understand better the ebb and flow of energy between us and our communicators at all times. Spirit will work very hard to come down into our plane to work with us and to communicate, however there is a vast difference between the energetic state the realm of Spirit, and the physical nature of the earth plane of our existence.

The realm of Spirit is a place of easy communication, where through and emotion can be transferred readily and without the need for many of the excess of methods of expression that we use every day of our lives. Imagine then the difficulty faced by all our loved ones and Spirit communicators when they return back down to our own denser and physical vibrational level of existence. Many of the methods of communication that we rely upon almost without thought for our information must once again be manifest through the mind of the Medium, and the Medium must also learn to be responsible for interpreting this communication not only accordingly, but also accurately.

Relying solely on Spirit to make the full transition to this realm is not only an unrealistic goal but is also a sign of sloppy or lazy attempts at communication. While we all like events in our life to be easy, we must learn to rise above our human need to be the centre of attention and appreciate the profound effort already in place by our friends in Spirit. To idly sit back and wait for them to come to you is not only lazy, but disrespectful Mediumship and will rarely produce any good connection to spirit. As a result the quality of communication suffers.

We must always be mindful of the miracle that is represented by the existence of Spirit communication and work equally as hard from our side of the connection.

Can you imagine attempting to telephone someone who does not want to get up from their couch or seat to pick up and answer? If so then you can see the need for the medium to actively become involved in working to establish an improved and more substantial link. Spirit will always give one hundred and fifty percent in their communication. If you are not receiving it, then it is because you either do not know how to, or you are not trying to do as much as you can.

Every medium must attempt to meet Spirit half way in their attempt to achieve spirit communication. The process to do so often requires little else than working at improving our skills for extending our awareness out to Spirit. Once again, like many of the issues covered within this book, these may seem simple but are far from easy. Hard work and dedication to the service that we are hoping to provide is the only way to build up our knowledge and experience.

Eventually, given time, patience and continued practice under the tutelage of an experienced Medium and development circle or group, you will begin to make progress in receiving information. It will take years to develop and understand all that you receive so have no misconceptions or pre-conceived notions. Just be open to the possibilities and if you are truly sincere in your efforts, Spirit will support you in all that you do.

As you can imagine, everything that a Medium is required to do and work with can and is a mammoth task to accomplish with every message delivered. In every single communication the medium is required to work, and to gather information, then to process and strengthen the links that we make. Finally they are then responsible for filtering everything that comes through into a form recognised by the sitter.

Fortunately no medium is ever truly alone when they work to deliver messages of love and support from those who can no longer be with us in this physical life. There are many in Spirit who continually works with and for us on our behalf, specifically our Spirit Guides and teachers.

Help and Guidance

In every aspect of our lives, whether spiritual or mundane, we come into contact with those who are there to help, align, encourage and promote our development. Oftentimes this is as a by-product of choices we make and paths which we tread as we grow and move forward in our daily lives. From our parents, to the many teachers we have in school, to work colleagues, friends, authors, journalists and even those who sometimes fight against us along the way. There is always an opportunity to evaluate our progress and to take time to learn from any given situation as we travel our path. All we have to do is to be open and receptive to the messages and truths being presented to us.

This is relatively easy in the physical sense. But what about on our own spiritual pathway, where does the learning and guidance come in? Certainly there are many people in the world to whom we turn for some measure of assistance or belief when we feel the need to invoke a change, but what about all the times in between?

What about in the quiet spaces between the trials and stresses, where our physical self is apparently content with its lot and does not feel the need to reach out for a greater meaning or purpose other than a simple task at hand. Does the learning and progression of our spirit stop? Are there no teachers in Spirit or within the Divine universe that help or guild us forward?

Of course there are, and they work equally as hard for us even when we are unaware of their actions or their presence. We have many Guides and teachers who come into and out of our lives almost as readily as those we meet in our physical life.

Some come forward to help us with personal issues or matters that they were once connected to. Others are members of our family, or friends, who see us struggling with the day to fay issues in our lives and who just want to help out or heal us from our pains and worries. Many more are working 'behind the scenes' to open doors and encourage not only our spiritual development but also our personal growth and continued existence. They may be old friends from ages past or simply great masters or scholars who wish to share their knowledge and have chosen us as the vessel through which to do it. There is truly no end of possibilities toward sudden inspiration or learning when Spirit decides to come forward and work with or complement our own abilities.

This does not mean that everything you do and say is spiritually inspired, however.

Assistance and not Assertion

Throughout the years I have met and worked with many individuals who put almost everything that occurs in their life down to the intervention of Spirit and give themselves little or no credit for most of what they accomplish. Likewise they also then accept little or no personal responsibility for when things go wrong.

There is a warning to be noted here about becoming too reliant and dependant on over-inflating the work and the motivation for Spiritual assistance, as well as the belittling of your own hard efforts and endeavours.

Remember that a great deal, and probably most of what you do, is powered by and comes from you and that higher aspect of yourself that is the Spirit within. The things we do and accomplish may have been assisted by Spirit, particularly in the early days of an ideas creation, such as through the sowing of a few notions or seeds in your mind. However you can always guarantee that your spirit assistance would have stopped then and there when you picked up the reins, for this is your journey, your path, and they would never want to interfere and over-run your life.

That is simply not what they do and certainly not in the best interest of either yours or anyone around you. If Spirit were to move in and assert control over all that you did then it would lead to a false sense of perspective in what you can achieve on your own and would mean that you are being neglected of the one things that you have come to this life for, to learn from all that you do, regardless of whether or not the outcome was positive or negative.

Can you imagine for a minute what it would feel like to break a world record? You would be joyous, elated and on such a personal high that you deserve to be proud of all that work and all that effort that got you to that place. Now imagine that you find out you had two big spiritual athletes holding you up and essentially dragging you along the track. How would that victory feel now and what would it do to you? It would destroy not only your confidence in yourself, but tarnish everything that got you to that point and all that you would do from that moment forward. You would lose your will to drive forward, to challenge, to improve and most importantly, to live. Above all else, our loved ones want to see us live a rich and fulfilling life under our own steam and through our own achievements, albeit with a little nudge here and there where appropriate to keep us on the path.

Rest assured Spirit may point in a direction, give you a push and an indication of what you need to do to heal and improve, but the rest is up to you and you alone. If you do not try then they likewise will, but when you embrace your path the Spirit and all those who work with you will be elated and then they will do what they can to ease the passage to your goal, but you are still the primary force for completion and success.

Guiding the Way

In additional to teachers and family, each and every one of us has some form of guide in Spirit to help with direction and how best to make use of the talents and abilities which we have. Like all of those in spirit who aid us they are not there to overshadow us, or alter our free will, but are to support and nurture our spiritual growth and development when we do choose to go down that path.

For each and every one of us, that particular guide, or aspect of that guide that we are able to accept for ourselves can and invariably will change throughout our life. For most of us, these guides may the perceived form of what we are capable of understanding. Often these are icons and images of what we consider to be of spiritual significance and which resonate with us on our own personal vibrational level. Very often our guides come to us as such as Shaman, Magicians, Monks, Wolves or other mystical and spiritually relevant beings and figures. This occurs simply because that is what we can relate to in terms of what we want to be guided by and very often Spirit will want to work with us and adopt the images and iconography that we relate to the most in order to be accepted by us and get their guidance through in the most direct way.

I have a love of Wolves, it has been with me all my life and I cannot explain it at all. Whenever I am asked to think of an animal…'poof!' in a cloud of smoke there is a big wolf with soulful yellow eyes. The same when I meditate and am asked to think of an animal ….'poof!'… there he is again. Always watching, doing little but often just the very presence of the creature is soothing and I feel as though I belong. I understand that this is merely the shape and form that this energy takes in the moment to allow me to access a certain level of my own subconscious. Essentially the guide is using the wolf energy to connect to me in a way that I am comfortable with.

It is important to never forget that although we are spirit, we are Spirit in a physical life with physical limitation placed upon it. Although our guides exist, they do so in their own state of being which we manifest in our minds either consciously or subconsciously to fit our own ideal. When we see them it is through our meditations and our techniques of communication and rarely, if ever, in direct manifestation save perhaps during a very advanced Physical Mediumship séance. During this a guide or spirit contact may form by making use of the raised energy and vibrations within the room to manipulate and manifest a shape for itself.

The fact is that we regularly only really see our guides within our mind. Does that make them more or less real? Of course not, but we must always remember that our perceptions are tempered by this physical world. We should not let our physical and mental limitations prevent us from identifying what is and is not actually manifest within our guides, or what they are here to accomplish with us.

Within this lies one of the challenges of our physical life and our own journey toward a more developed spiritual existence. We must learn to break apart from all our physical limitations and seek what is truly spiritual in all things, particularly from and with regard to our Guides.

Respect your Guide

We need to always remember that, despite having lived one or more existences, these guides are now beings of Spirit who have agreed to work with and alongside us for however long to aid us in our development. They may have lived many lives, perhaps having even known and worked with us before in some other capacity.

They will have attained a great deal of wisdom through their own development, and have finally decided to bring that to us this time around again to enable us to do the same. They may have been our fathers, mothers, sons, daughters, loved ones, friends, confidants or inspiring figures in any number of previous incarnations. They may be with us forever or for only a set period of time until we have learned what we need from that individual Spirit and it feels confident enough to let us go.

Always remember that they were once, like us, learning from their own life but they are now returned to the realm of spirit.

We should not be attributing them with our human characteristics and frailties. By all means work with them, learn from them and all they have to offer but do not place your own human values and attachments upon them for to do this is not only to discredit them, but to also disrespect what they have achieved and what they have come here to join us for.

Our guides and teachers wish nothing more than to aid us in understanding ourselves and to help us access the true universal and spiritual love that each and every one of us is capable of, and ask nothing more than we share that across the world.

I personally have never really met with a physical image or presence of any of my spiritual guides or teachers, or at least not that I remember. I have no problem at all with this and can readily accept that they work equally as well with or without the validation of who, what and when they were. It may be one or two guides and they may be male or female, human or animal and I have no doubt that they will also more than likely have changed throughout the years. Ultimately I know and trust in their presence and when the time comes for them to present me with a physical image then it will happen. Until then, a mental communication only is more than enough.

Likewise my guides also do not appear to want or need to present themselves with any regularity of fanfare of trumpets to announce their presence. Over the years we have achieved a simple rapport that they use to let me know they are nearby simply by applying a very gentle pressure to my right temple (it is actually happening now as I write this so I better watch what I say about them!)

I attended a workshop with the amazing Glasgow medium Gordon Smith and he referred to these little moments of connection as your Guide's 'Calling Card'. This was a technique that resonated very deeply with me. I liked the symbolism of it as it also had a very business-like and no nonsense approach that suits my mind-set exactly. I can just imagine a Guide approach me with a brusque:

"Mr Scott, Hello, I'm your Guide, Here's my card. Now Meet Mrs Jones, she wants to speak to her daughter" Plain, simple, no-nonsense and direct to the point- I love it!

Let your Guides Guide!

It is important to remember that our Guides are so named because they work as best they can to guide us not only in our progression and development, but also within our actual Mediumship work when we are delivering messages.

They are there to help co-ordinate, organise and keep in order all the clamouring Spirits who may at any one time decide to step forward. In addition, they will direct and guide us toward the link we are required to go to next. They fulfil a very important purpose and so it is incredible vital that we both get to know how they work, and that we let them do their job as the go about their business.

Whenever we sit in meditation with intent to be of service and to work for Spirit, know that your Guide will be with you at all times and trust to this fact. You will need to work to get to know how your guide presents themselves, and how the guide wishes to interact with you, but persevere and it will come in time. All of this is purely down to you and can only come about through practiced meditation in a developing environment specifically geared toward learning the world of Spirit and learning to come to terms with and know yourself.

The more knowledge and experience you begin to take on board, the easier it becomes to let go of the various aspects of you until all that remains is that simple link between you, your guide, and the realm of Spirit.

Mediumship really is this simple. But never forget that simple and easy are two words often mixed up and misused. There really is a tremendous amount of work to do on ourselves and for our own personal and spiritual growth before we want to consider thinking of trying to help others through our mediumistic work. To do anything less than this is to be doing ourselves, the Spirit World, and those whom we hope to help the greatest of disservice.

Rest assured, when the times comes in your life for any of your teachers or guides to come forward and be known, they will be there instantly, and often even before you realise that you need them to be.

It is only by steadily working via a progressive and continued development, and challenging ourselves, that we truly begin to shape and form our psychic and spiritual faculties into anything that is useable either by ourselves, or by those in Spirit that we wish to serve.

Remember, there are no short cuts or lay-offs when it comes to ensuring that you remain in the best personal and spiritual condition you can be. The process of continued monitoring, assessment and training of oneself is always the key toward success in any field.

Personal Training

"The most important part of education is proper training"

Plato

Make no mistakes; there is little of greater importance, regardless of the field or discipline to which one applies their efforts, than the pursuit of a dedicated and lifelong approach to training and development of one's own abilities within the extents of the subject matter at hand.

At some point, everyone starts out as a novice on their chosen path with their own idea as to the reason behind things, but with little or no working knowledge of the how and the why. It is only through investigation, study, discovery and applying the information that we do find, that we are finally able to begin to understand the greater picture presented before us and in doing so we learn and grow in order to take the next steps along the route toward improvement.

Without achieving and manifesting a simple system of learning and understanding, realised through dedication and continual development, we make little genuine progress. There are times when we occasionally take small leaps forward over the gaps in our understanding, but in doing so we lack the wisdom and experience to fully comprehend the importance of what we have missed until, ultimately, we reach a point where we can go no further, for we have not yet understood where we came from.

It is not enough to simply know the steps to take in order to achieve a goal. One must live and experience each and every part of the process and to allow themselves the time that they need in order that they may absorb the requisite level of understanding for them to develop. For almost all of us, this is realised through simple, stage by stage, training in whatever we choose to study. In finding the starting point and working forward, we can honestly appraise ourselves with regard to where we are along the chosen path as no training is ever truly wasted, for even that which suits us the least and teaches us even less still tells us something about either the subject, or ourselves and how we want to progress from this point forward.

Lifetime Learning

Yet, development is not only for the novice and the unlearned. Even for the most dedicated and experienced there is benefit to go back and look anew, with older and wiser eyes, upon where they once were. From personal experience in all aspects of life, what we see is usually a revelation to our senses to say the least.

Genuine dedication, development and training for learning not only permits is to progress, but it also prepares us to receive information from all sources and not simply from our own experiences. In looking toward increasing our understanding of all that we can achieve, we open ourselves up to the views and methodologies of others. In doing so we are able to share knowledge across all extents and boundaries that may otherwise have remained closed to us.

In looking into and accepting the methods that we all use, we pool our resources of knowledge together and work toward a common goal of furthering the knowledge base of the matter at hand for future development, progress and reflection. This is the true gift that is received by all of those who take up and path of learning and understanding. They become forever entwined in the destiny of that discipline and in their own time will forge new benchmarks, attain greater and newer standards, and establish new starting points for all of those who follow on behind us.

Within the field of Mediumship there can be no doubt that training and development is vital to our initial and continued growth. But this is also true for any subject that we choose to study. Study provides us with knowledge, understanding, and the workings of that subject in order that we may better comprehend and utilise what we know to our best advantage. In doing so we preserve the progress we and others make, and serve to pave the way for future generations to do the same.

In making a dedicated commitment to actual learning we are working toward improvement through a system or means of study. From this vantage point we can easily step out of the dark shadows of ignorance and blind searching, and reach out for assistance to those teachers around us who have walked the same path. In doing so we realise that we are not alone in this world, but that there are indeed others like us with the same motivations and goal. From these others we can exchange both knowledge and experience to not only avoid the pitfalls and hazards, but to ensure that we provide the best level of service whenever we are asked to step up to the plate, take some responsibility and put our faith in Spirit and in our own self-awareness.

Losing Oneself

I often think that the workers in Spirit, and certainly the power that is the divine source of all things, must truly be in possession of a wonderful sense of humour and irony. As a medium, this becomes most apparent when you begin to understand that a major factor in the mechanics behind making mediumistic connections is to lose your connection to yourself in order make a connection to others. While this may seem contrary, particularly after you spend so long trying to become familiar with your physical self and your own emotional and mental responses, it is a vital part of knowing what sensations that you feel are coming from you, and what is coming through you from your communicator in Spirit.

As we work and we make the connections to Spirit, the various means of communication they provide may give us sensations, feelings, emotions or reactions to specific stimuli. A Spirit giving you the sensation of dizziness may have suffered from Vertigo, a sudden pain or numbness in a limb may indicate a disability they had in this life, or a sudden blurring of your vision may indicate eyesight related issues or poor vision, when you see the image of a house, was it the place where they lived?

Or are these perhaps just some of your own symptoms and memories? You will never know until you truly know and are aware of yourself, and you can distance your thoughts and emotions from your own physical and emotional self to present an empty mental canvas, as devoid of as many senses as possible, for you to welcome Spirit to come in and work with.

Every time I am about to work, I meditate and focus on myself. I make myself aware of each and every part of my body systematically before I go into a short meditation to link to my guides and then to those waiting in Spirit to step forward. As I feel the guides move in, I allow that small part of my consciousness which contains my own needs or wants and desires to step back and not interfere with the communication process. This is not entirely unlike entering a trance state but involves no deep meditation or giving up of control to another. By simply stepping back a little in my mind I can be completely in control of my body and my actions, but give room for the Spirit who communicates to work more easily.

In losing the parts of me that are not required, they are not there to block or interfere and so when Spirit steps in, I can trust that the information is true and accurate and focus on the task at hand. To deliver the message as given directly from the person in Spirit to be relayed the loved one before me. All my own personal issues are replaced by a simple request to serve both Spirit and the person they wish to relay a message to, and I remind myself that I am merely the conduit and means of communication, nothing more.

Listening with Responsibility

In between the actions of Spirit to communicate, our guides to assist and the medium to act as the focus and delivery of information there is one final and very important part of the link that is often overlooked.

The sitter and receiver of the message must engage with the process fully and completely.

When a recipient is allowing their energy and connection to both the medium and the contact to flow, provided that they are an open-minded and attentive source, the final part of the miracle of communication is allowed to take place. In contrast, where the sitter is closed off or not fully open to the process, it becomes very difficult for either the medium or the contact to make proper communication.

There is truly nothing worse than trying to deliver a message to a recipient who sits, their posture defensive, arms crossed and demanding all with a 'prove it' attitude. In such instances, the medium cannot help but be affected by the negative energy flowing from them and it serves to merely impede the flow of information to and from spirit.

Every recipient must be aware that the process of communication is not theirs by right, but is a genuine gift from their loved ones who truly want nothing more than to make a genuine and loving connection. It cannot be demanded and it cannot be wrenched from the Spirit connection.

Often when our loved ones come close, and they recognise who they wish to speak to, the communication flows so easily. When that loved one suddenly becomes defensive, their energy changes and the Spirit fails to recognise that they are with the correct recipient. This is understandable for they had perhaps never seen them act in such a way before. Both the medium and spirit begin to doubt and so the information slows as they try to re-establish that they did indeed have the correct individual.

You can imagine the confusion in yourself if you met an old and trusted friend who suddenly became defensive in your presence. How uncomfortable that would be and how quickly it would make you end that conversation. For Spirit it is no different.

When we are about to receive a Spirit communication we should not come to this wonderful moment and gift of love from the position of someone who demands all. We should be ready to give both faith and love back and to accept the potential for that truth of contact to be realised. Then, and only then, can we truly be part of the moment where our Spirits link once again. At this time an old friend is once again permitted to reach out to us and touch our very heart and soul.

Chapter 4

DEVELOPING MEDIUMSHIP

Be Understanding

FOR THOSE WHO DO decide to investigate and examine their capabilities to work either Mediumistically or psychically, it is vital that they go into the process with an open mind that is a blank slate. You really must be prepared to put all of your expectations and past experiences behind you and be prepared to work as though you are a complete novice, ignorant of all knowledge achieved prior to this point.

Before you set out on deciding to develop your mediumistic ability be very aware of your motives and intention. Are you doing this because of a desire to want to help others, or for your own personal development and gain? Be honest, and remember that Spirit will know even if you do not, and they are quite definite in which of these types of individual that they can and do prefer to work with.

I remember attending a charity evening run by one of the local churches in my area. After a demonstration it is quite natural for some, if not most, of the audience to come up and ask you a few things but I remember that on this particular evening I was approached by a younger woman from the audience. Her manner was not rude but certainly abrupt.

"How much do you get paid for these charity events?" she asked "I'm just wondering because I kind of get things and I go to a lot of these nights and go to see these mediums all the time. I can do Cards and stuff and I was wondering about bringing in some extra money. I really do get things you know!"

Initially I was a little taken aback by her question. Clearly whatever information she got and wherever it came from, she did not truly 'get it' when it came down to working with Spirit.

When I informed her that I was not actually being paid for the event, on account of it being a Charity Evening she shrugged, appeared to lose interest, and walked away.

True spiritual work is an energetic exchange, yes there are times when a person's services can be paid for, however this is for the value of the individuals time invested in doing so and not necessarily for the skills used. Simply pursuing a career in working for Spirit solely to earn money is rarely successful. Spirit are just not interested in working with anyone who has so little regard for the importance of their work, compassion for the recipient, and respect for the communicator, that they put themselves and their desire for capital gain above all else.

There can be many misconceptions with regard to what Mediumship is and how it is to be used, particularly given the televised boom in our world today with regard to the paranormal and the unexplained. Much of this is nothing more than entertainment desired to bring in ratings and spread moments of fearful enjoyment in much the same way as a fairground Ghost House or Train does, and should not be taken at all seriously.

Anyone who wishes to emulate what they see on television by working on their medium abilities will always be highly disappointed with the result. The realm of Spirit has its focus directed toward a much bigger picture than any of us may be aware of and we must remember that everything we encounter in our lives contains a greater message and task for each of us.

Mediumship is Healing

True Mediumship and work for spirit is always done with the intent to serve, to heal, and is working within the light of Spirit both inside us and for those around us. There is no darkness in Spirit, only true and genuine love for our Spirit nature.

Regardless of where you look in the history of genuine and true work for Spirit there is always a focus upon the need for healing in each and every event or message. To work for Spirit is to embrace this part of ourselves that is able to make contact with the spirit and soul of all around us to give healing and hope to the world. This is the path of the Medium and to take it up requires not only a desire to work, but also an open-ness and awareness of the human frailty that is evident in each and every one of us. We all, in some aspects need to heal. For some this is done physically, for others this is accomplished through words, thoughts and belief.

Before we heal others however, we need to know how to face up to and heal our own issues, insecurities, needless desires and want for control of everything that occurs in our lives. Many of the problems that we face are self-generated and we need to be willing to work on and release what we often do not wish to.

Before we begin working for others we need to be able to first work for and care for ourselves.

You need to Work

As you begin to develop your Mediumship, be ready to work on yourself and mend a great deal of the problems and issues that will inevitably arise along the way. Take things slowly and steadily and do not try to jump or leapfrog your way forward in your progress without first fully understanding each stage along on our journey.

You will be required to listen to your heart and soul with a great deal of honesty and be required to overcome your own Ego as you challenge your beliefs in not only the connections that you make but also the information that you receive. At every stage you will likewise need to prevent yourself from becoming overconfident, from being held back or waylaid in making progress by clinging to past success or failure. You may find that you will have to overcome personal prejudices and challenge views that you never thoughts existed, and you will face the doubts and fears that you create in yourself time and time again as to whether or not this is the right path for you.

In the end only you can rise up to face and answer these issues. Deep down, in the core of your own Spirit, you will know the truth and will be required to be responsible for all the choices you make on your journey.

There is so much more to being a medium than just delivering messages. There is a universe of knowledge and understanding, and an eternal resource of Spiritual guidance and teaching that have been passed down to us in this life through some highly gifted Mediums over the years. As you develop you will begin to understand the extents of responsibility that is being placed upon you. You will be required to research and review the past in order to understand the future, you will invariably attend workshops and look for other ways to progress and continue developing new skills and methods of working.

As a medium you should always strive to provide the very best and most accurate information possible, it is what we are required to do in order to be what we are with any degree of success in giving someone a message that heals and brings hope from a loved one. Anything less is a dis-service and does not give the requisite level of importance to the wonderful truth that we are eternal and our Spirit never dies.

Forget the television and the media and focus on the message behind the move visual aspects of Mediumship, the service to the divine, and to the realm of Spirit and the great Love that binds it all together.

Be part of something

Anyone who wishes to develop both themselves and their ability has many options to choose from; however the best results always occur when we are able to develop in the presence of like-minded people. Learning any type of new skills or improving upon existing one is always very daunting and requires that we work out-with our comfort zones.

On any journey of self-discovery we will always need either guidance or encouragement from those who have gone before us and who have made either the correct decisions or the wrong ones in getting to where they are.

Finding a good spiritual teacher and inspirer is no mean task, there is a minefield of information available at our fingertips these days and one only has to type 'Mediumship training' into a search engine to be hit with about a million results and options. If you do not believe me, try it. .

This is once again an example of how we, as human beings, can make things difficult for ourselves in the long run. The best place to start is not necessarily by searching online and scouring the world for the best teachers at the best locations, but by searching locally.

Trust me, if Spirit want you to be working with any of the

most well-known mediums or spiritual workers from across the world, they will open doors for you to make it happen, you just need to be patient and to give yourself time to find your place and role in the work that you are doing, or may be about to.

Almost every town or area has at least one Spiritualist Church or personal and spiritual development group set up. Most of these advertise within both the local and national press so narrow down the field of where you look to where you live. Many of the local churches and groups out there, whether they are affiliated to larger and well-established organisation or not, are often the best place to begin working toward developing your mediumistic abilities.

They are generally open, friendly, places and will have members who have gathered many years' experience working for and on behalf of the Spirit realm. The church will be dedicated to serving both Spirit and their congregation and always are an essential first point of call for anyone with an interest in learning about working for Spirit.

The church or group will most certainly run regular weekly nights and services where you can go along, speak to and meet mediums of all types, experiences and specialisms. Within these small groups and churches you can truly see the power of Spirit at work, and the unbelievable amount of healing and consideration that our loved ones still wish to give to us as they bring words of comfort and hope to so many.

They may run an open development circle where it is possible for you to attend and sit and learn to meditate, gain experience in becoming accustomed to working with Spirit, and where you will receive education and guidance in all aspects of Mediumship, Spiritualism, and most importantly on what you should and should not be doing in order to make progress.

Be Dedicated

Everything that we do in life, particularly those endeavours in which we want to succeed or which mean so very much to us, requires us to dedicate a significant amount of time and effort to its practice. When we naturally want to improve and progress and become better at our chosen tasks we must hold strong that old adage that 'practice makes perfect'. It should come as no surprise then to be told that the training and development of one's psychic or mediumistic abilities is no different. It requires a great deal of regular and dedicated hard work before we being to see the even the first fruits of our labours.

Although we may be born with the limited and basic function to make use of these abilities, they cannot develop properly unless we actively set out to work with them and determine where our own capabilities, strengths and weaknesses may lie. The progress of the spirit, the understanding of our spiritual being, and the development of our ability to communicate with the Spirit world is no less different. To lead a life where one chooses to develop in a spiritual fashion will demand that you must be prepared to accept the requirement and discipline needed for daily practice in order to keep our minds and hearts open to the possibilities.

Our spiritual muscles are no less different than any other physical one, requiring a regular regime of exercises and attention to maintaining their peak condition. For some this is done through meditation and prayer, for others it is through actions and commitment to ideals or philosophies. There is no true and genuine 'one' way to progress, for each method is entirely personal and applies only to that particular individual. What works for us will not necessarily work for others, for each and every one of us is unique, only sharing a few of the most basic common similarities. Just as some of us are runners, others swim and others play team sports to keep ourselves in top shape, not all of us will be able to be a medium, but we may be a healer or teacher, philosopher, writer or any of the other ways in which our Spirit power can be manifest.

So, like our physical fitness, our spiritual fitness can come only from our own drive and effort. To be true to ourselves and our beliefs by putting genuine effort into practice is one of the greatest gifts that we can give ourselves. To successfully meet the needs of what we require to grow and learn and, for the benefit of all those others around us and in the realm of Spirit, to move forward as a spiritual being is one of the fundamental aspects of honouring and understanding not only our own spirituality, but also ourselves.

No matter what path you take in life be it physical, mental or spiritual, do it with honesty and to the fullest commitment for the betterment of yourself and all that you come into contact with. Be dedicated and always question your reasons for following your spiritual path. If you are truly happy with the answer you find then keep working toward your progress.

Remember, there are no shortcuts to be made on your own personal spiritual journey. Take your time to become familiar with all aspects of your work and then, with dedication and perseverance to working for Spirit, take each step as it comes.

PART 2

Working for Spirit

Chapter 5

To be a Medium

The Medium's Role

WHAT DOES IT MEAN to be a medium?

In the very simplest terms, a Medium works for Spirit. Their purpose is to act as a communicator and focus between the divine power of our loved ones, friends and acquaintances who have passed beyond this earthly existence and who wish to be well, and to let us know that they are still with us, and always will be.

There is however so much more to being a medium than simply delivering messages or channelling healing thoughts. Not to take anything away from these fundamental aspects of Spiritual belief, but these are simply the evidential and public face of Mediumship and represents only a tiny fraction of what it truly means to work on behalf of the Spirit World.

Each of us who chooses to develop and work for spirit will find ourselves following in the footsteps of a legacy of spiritual pioneers, educators and motivators. Dedicated individuals who have not only opened the eyes of the world to the spirit realm, but who did so often at great personal cost. These individuals all fought and worked to make the world aware of the existence of the spirit world and the simple truth that we are indeed eternal.

All who work as mediums must carry aloft the legacy of the

past and seek to deliver it into the future, with the appropriate level of dedication and responsibility equal to that given to it by these early pioneers.

Reasons and Motives

As we come into contact with our own Spirit, and we begin to acknowledge and tap into that awareness and connection to the Spirit world, we often find that there begins to open up within us a drive or purpose that we were previously unaware of.

For anyone who wishes to be either a medium or any worker for Spirit, the motives must be coming from that Spirit within and not from any other external desire or source.

Always continue to ask yourself, and answer with utmost honesty:

- Do I fully recognise and understand the nature of this work?
- Can I honestly be a free and unbiased channel for Spirit?
- Am I in the right place to follow this path right now?
- Is my purpose here to serve Spirit?
- Am I willing to give up what I think I know, and to begin learning?
- Do I trust myself?
- Am I willing to trust to Spirit?
- What do I expect from this?

An uncertain response does not indicate that you are incapable of development, but may mean that you are not yet ready at this moment to commit to the process.

To work for Spirit requires not only the deepest commitment, but also an awareness of oneself and the necessary sacrifices that we may need to make in order to be of service. Simply wishing to be a medium does not make you one. There is first and foremost a great deal of personal work to do. This may involve releasing aspects of our past and dedicating our self to look upon and forgive many things that we have experienced.

Above all, we must be open to personal change and be capable of listening and learning.

Learn from Spirit

To be a medium is to be of service not only to Spirit, but to all those who come into our life. It requires one to have a very deep commitment to all that they do and all that they experience and to seek to rise above the purely mundane things. It requires that we all strive to work toward understanding the intricate way in which life and all its facets connect together to create a thing of beauty, just as the minerals and pressure in the earth can create the most beautiful of gemstones.

A medium, be they spirit communicators or healers, should always be working on themselves to maintain a view of the world that is geared to look at the greater picture of things. In order to be of service to others we must first be able to at least see beyond the overall implication of individual events in every aspects of our own life, for everything that we create is relative to our experience.

A great many times this only becomes apparent long after we have gone through the process of reconciliation of the past and, with time, we can look back in hindsight and see the small connections and co-incidences that have led us to where we are today.

We are, in truth, only really able to learn from the events that we encounter and learn to overcome throughout our lives, be they either positive or negative. What matters most is the manner in which we deal with our lives on a daily basis, and how we take responsibility to lead our lives forward from any given point.

This is, naturally, a lifelong process and will always be so. To stop learning or challenging oneself is to invite stagnation and severance from the world at large. Like any professional, to work for spirit you must always be willing to remain active in your studies, pursuit and understanding of the world of spirit and the methods in which you interact with it.

We all change frequently throughout our lives, we age and our bodies change, our point of view and perspectives are altered by the events that we encounter and the direction that we choose to take. There are very few in this world who can claim to be exactly the same person that they were several years ago. As human beings we are easily distracted and affected by the physical world and all within it, yet we must always remember that it is our physical form that is limited to and remains in this physical life.

Our spiritual self has the capacity to be untarnished and free of the limitations put on our lives by the physical world, but once again we must work to ensure that it does so. As mediums we must learn to accept that we can do only what we are able to do at any given time, and then release and let go that which we cannot. In doing so we become free from our own restriction and prejudices and will always be able to learn in an active and fluid way.

Spirit uses all it can

I can remember travelling to a Spiritualist Church one night by car and I was listening to the radio as I drove the two hours or so it took to reach the church. The trip was generally uneventful and I can recall changing channels on the radio several times to get away from the numerous news reports and stories that broke into the normal music. Eventually I gave up on the radio, connected my iPhone to the car and spent the remainder of the journey listening to some of my favourite songs.

Everything seemed normal that evening and the church service started well, I gave a short address and philosophy and soon my demonstration of Mediumship started. Immediately I picked up the presence of first one, then more, spiritual contacts coming forward to communicate. What made this evening different however was that they were all either young persons or children, I remember thinking that getting so many young communicators through in one evening was unusual but put it aside and continued to work.

After the service, on the way home, I turned the radio on once again and was just in time for the end of the news report. During the report there were several separate articles about either children or young persons' being missing, injured, and also sadly killed in accidents, road crashes or disasters around the world.

It was then I realised that this was the same news article that I had heard that evening on the way to church before I turned off the radio. Clearly it had registered somewhere in my subconscious and had affected the operating level of my Mediumship that particular evening. In hearing these tragic stories, my thoughts had gone out to touch on the energetic level of Spirit for those who had passed at a younger age that particular evening. Can it be any wonder then that these were the first individuals to step forward and be known? Perhaps their parents and family had heard the news as well and their thoughts too were linking out to Spirit in remembrance of their children.

Either way, it highlighted to me just how easily we can be affected by the world around us, and how our Mediumship can be altered and directed by our thoughts. It also proved to me beyond any doubt that if Spirit wants to get a message through, then they will. I am sure that I was supposed to hear that news in order to make those links because the loved ones in Spirit so desperately wanted to get a message that they are well and still love them back to those who needed to hear it.

Success and Failure

There will be moments of what we perceive to be both success and failure on this journey of Spiritual development and Mediumship. Allow each of these to be encountered and then released. Do not hold on to either of these moments as anything other than the learning tools that they are. Make note of what you need to and then move forward.

A medium must always try to release and let go. It is never correct to become caught up in seeking praise for success and all we get correct, likewise we should never truly be locked into punishing themselves for everything that does not work.

Never forget that the best work done for Spirit is completed then and there, and it is then let go and released. Your work is not truly finished, just that one part of it that you have completed within that single moment of time. There is more to come just around the next turn in your journey and you should be ready to face it afresh and unaffected by the events of the past.

Stay true to the principles of your work and the standards that you know are true. Always uphold all the responsibilities of your position and remember that that you have been given an opportunity to serve. Then, undertake your work and strive to do all that you can with the skills and tools that you have at your disposal.

For communicators this means delivering your message, for healers this is channelling healing. That is truly all that Spirit ask of you, and in trusting to them and all your guides and teachers, in giving them the appropriate level of service and dedication to your work, they will ensure that you are assisted at every bend and turn in the road ahead.

Speaking for Spirit

The role of the medium is not simply that of a messenger. Every medium is also an important ambassador for the Spiritualist faith, the Spirit realm, and all those who work with us in our work. It is vital to remember that mediums, regardless of their experience or ability are constantly judged not only on their words, but also their actions and intentions. All that they undertake within their spiritual work has the potential to impact upon not only the view of the world toward themselves, but also toward the future attitudes and ideas of our society toward the progress of Spiritualism.

As you can imagine, choosing to work on behalf of Spirit brings with it additional responsibilities. We should never forget that we say and do within our role have so much potential to positively or negatively affect the lives of so many people and persons with whom we come into contact with. Those who come forward to work with us from the spiritual realm have many options open to them, they may choose to speak directly to us, inspire us to write or to give evidence, or even may directly communicate via utilising our physical self in trance to give account of their teachings.

Knowing the difference between what comes directly from spirit through these various states of focus and levels of communication, and what may actually be coming from some deep rooted part of ourselves, is vital for all of us who work this closely with our spirit guides, teachers and helpers.

This is why knowing our own self and becoming familiar with our own mind, body and spirit is so very important to consistently work at, maintain and understand. We are, as mediums, being tasked with the responsibility of giving over information in a clear, concise and unobstructed manner that is free from any of our own perceptions. Yes we will be required to interpret the more unusual and abstract forms of symbolism and communication, but it needs to be done so without our own logical minds becoming involved. In order to do to the best of our abilities must to be able to detach our active thoughts and logic from any subject matter in order that we can properly deliver the information that comes through.

As you can imagine, this requires a great deal of trust and this can only come into being through our practice and familiarity with sitting, meditating on ourselves and Spirit, and through getting to know not only our guides and helpers, but also what comes from within ourselves

Trust in Spirit's Knowledge.

I recall working at a charity evening with two of my fellow mediums and on that particular night, I had already stood up to address the audience and had given off some messages, one in particular to a whole family from their father who had passed away some years ago. In this he thanked them all for a poem that they had placed in his coffin and asked me to relay that he had read it and he would never forget the words.

When I had sat down and one of my colleagues had stood up to work on delivering messages from the Spirit connections she was making, I became aware of a tiny gnawing in the back of my mind that this gentleman had not yet gone away. Despite me trying to move out of his energy, he was becoming very insistent and still wanted to speak to both me and his family. It was becoming obvious that the more I tried to withdraw from him, the stronger he tried to communicate and I could pick up some words playing over and over in my mind. Rather than continuing to fight it, I decided to open up to what this gentleman wanted me to communicate.

I sent my thoughts out to my guide who assured me that everything was all right, and that the gentleman had something very important that he needed to get across, but had not wished to do so from a public platform. He had, in fact, no intention of speaking but had wanted to give me something to write down and pass on.

Fortunately for me that evening we had a psychic artist along with us to this event and I asked him if I could borrow his pen and paper for a minute. He obliged and I began writing down all the words that came into my mind. This was a definite first for me as I could feel this gentleman's Spirit draw so very near and while I was fully in control of the entire event and the writing process, the words just seemed to flow out of me and into the paper. It felt as though he was guiding not only my mind but my hand, and slowly the lines began to form into a short poem.

The flow of information and communication within the poem continued for three small verses and when it finished I signed it off an unusually shaped capital 'R' at the bottom of the last line. The spirit gentleman, who had up until then not actually given me any indication of a name asked me to pass this to the family and, during the interval break I went up to their table and, only the spirit gentleman's daughter being there, presented her with it and said that it had just been given to me and if they wanted to inquire about it then they could come speak to me after the Mediumship that evening.

I remember seeing the mother of the family come back to the table, along with a few more family members a few minutes later and they all looked over at me rather strangely. Putting this to the back of my mind I refocused my thoughts on the task at hand and my colleagues and I continued with the evening.

At the end of the night, the girl came back up to me, her excitement was evident and she told me that the poem I had given her had mimicked some of sentiment that was in the poem they had put in their fathers coffin when it had lain in state in the funeral parlour. She then went on to say that what this gentleman had given me to write also contained reference to an event that occurred in the funeral home the last time her mother had seen her father. Yet what had moved her mother more than anything else was the odd shaped 'R' at the bottom, as this was identical to her father, Robert's, own style of signature.

I can tell you that she and her family were not the only ones taken aback that evening. I was not only amazed but also very humbled and so grateful to have been of service to the particular gentleman in spirit, and his family who had still been grieving their loss at that time.

Since then, I have never had another spontaneous writing experience such as that one. When I look back on it I am convinced that it was genuinely another example of Spirit making sure that the right person was in the right place at the right time to deliver what needed to be done, and in the manner that it required to be given.

What would have happened I wonder if I had just ignored the sensations and the need to put down on paper the incredible message of love and hope that this gentleman was asking me to relay?

If I had allowed my logical brain to kick in that evening and thought to myself "Steven you don't do written messages" then that moment would have been lost, perhaps never to have been repeated again.

When Spirit have a message that they want to get through, then they will do it not only with whatever they have at hand, but may even make use of some of the most clever and abstract methods to do so. All it takes is for you to work with the skills and abilities that you have as often as you can, to hone and practice and permit Spirit to make use of every aspect of yourself when they communicate through you, and to trust.

Responsible Action

We must all learn to trust completely that Spirit will work to get that message across using all means at their disposal and in the manner in which it needs to be given. However never forget that each of us is also personally responsible for the delivery of this message, and this is in no small way a one of the most important aspects of our ability as a medium. It is no use in receiving information of support and love if, in the delivery of it, you undo all the good that it will bring.

Being a speaker for spirit requires that you remain open and understanding of both the energy of your communicator, and the energy of the recipient and those around them. We must be aware and cognizant of the impact and effects that our communications have on others and accept full responsibility for the consequences of all our words. Putting the blame back onto the communicator and claiming that you only say what they tell you to say is just no excuse for poor behaviour or language during the delivery of a message.

When you speak for Spirit, you must listen to not only what you get through but also the manner in which it is given. Sometimes an explanation of the Spirits demeanour and means of communication in advance of delivering the message is essential. It not only identifies another aspect of their character, but then allows you to deliver the message without the need to emulate or mimic the spirit communicators own characteristics, particularly of these are not suitable for the public platform.

There will be times when Spirit presents you with very sensitive and extremely personal information that they wish to be passed on. This is particularly true when their actions in the past have caused pain that is yet to be released by the intended receiver and, now free of their physical restraints and once more having access to their true Spirit, they can see the hurt that they have caused, and the effect it still has upon someone they cared for.

It is never appropriate to just shout out everything that Spirit gives you and every Medium should always retain responsibility for their words. It is wrong to openly release information to everyone around that is highly confidential for the one person just because Spirit told you about it. Remember that the individual Spirit may be desperate to get either their apologies, or even their forgiveness, through and simply because they put it to you, you must choose when and how to release that information. If in doubt always ask for the recipient to speak to you later, it will be better for all concerned and ensures that you stay professional in your approach to the work that you do.

Always be respectful and mindful of the hurt that may still be there and treat everyone, Spirit and Recipient alike, with the greatest of respect.

There is never, nor will there ever be, any need for a Spirit communicator to deliver and communicate a message that is seething with blame, ill feeling or improper intent. No Spirit energy will ever say or do anything detrimental to the receiver, even if those individuals were not particularly pleasant during the existence and time here on Earth. The energy and emotion that comes through during communication is positive, loving and does not set out to harm or cause and harm to the receiver.

Spirit has no such need for negative emotion and will manifest it only as a reference and no more. All the negativity, aggressiveness and poor attributes that we possess are purely our human aspect in this life and are never carried forward into the Spirit realm. All mediums must learn to remove themselves from the attributes being presented as past evidence, and learn to deal with these emotions accordingly as they pass through from Spirit, so as not to misinterpret these as the overall meaning and purpose of the communication.

The importance of responsibility and appropriate interpretation of information cannot be understated when any medium delivers a message to another person. You can readily spot a responsible medium within moments of their first communication. Any message will be informed, considerate and will deal not only with the provision of good evidence and characteristics of the communicator, but will also be relevant to current emotional and personal issues of the receiver. The message will be presented in such a way that it is delivered not only care and consideration, but with the respect and love that the Spirit communicator themselves would want to be giving to the receiver if they were able to do so themselves.

The Importance of Evidence

There is no doubt that the presentation of evidential Mediumship is a vital part of the process of Spirit communication, however we must also remember that the production of evidence it is not the only purpose of this communication. The presentation of evidence is merely a means of appeasing the human part of us that requires, if not demands, proof of identity and continued existence of our loved ones. The evidence does in fact, help to alleviate the doubt that we hold in our human heart with regard to the validity of the communication, and to provide proof of identity.

Just for a moment, consider a situation where communication with loved ones who had passed beyond this earthly life was accessed directly from within our own individual Spirit to those whom we had known and loved. In this situation, where we were able to speak directly through the power of our own loving connection to these individuals, would we require any evidence of their existence, or would we just communicate? If we could once again meet a loved parent, child or friend and just take that moment to once again know their presence and companionship, would we spend any time on demanding proof, or would we be overjoyed at the prospect of simply meeting them once again?

This is the situation faced by Spirit when they approach a medium and, perhaps for the first time in so long, have the opportunity to tell their loved ones that they are still cared for, that they are loved, and that they are being supported, healed or nurtured in every way possible. During communication, there can be multiple threads of information at any given time and it is up to the medium to control and direct the flow of information to the relevant person. All the while, the Spirit communicator knows that time is of the essence and they wish to get their information and messages of love through to those they have come to see.

Sometimes, the evidence proves to be part of these messages, for in giving evidence you also draw forward memories that have been shared and now can be relived, resulting in a moment of contact between Spirit and recipient as their energies meet in that moment. When this occurs, you can feel the sense of connection between the communicator and the receiver and it can be a truly wonderful and beautiful thing to behold the healing that occurs in such moments.

Evidential Greed or Evidential Need

There are times when a recipients desire for evidence appears to eclipse the importance of the message. When this occurs, those individual moments are lost for the receiver is so intent on demanding not just accurate evidence, but infallibly accurate evidence that is beyond all reasonable doubt that they often become disillusioned and disappointed with what is given to them. Oftentimes this is because their expectations of what they should receive have not been met or the facts, as they themselves remember the events to be, appear to be different. They often become closed to any other potential truth and refuse to even acknowledge anything else.

Herein lies a problem for any medium establishing a communication and link, for not every recipient is open and willing to accept unless it is in the format of their desire or on their terms, regardless of whether or not they possess full awareness of the facts.

Very often nowadays the human demand and need for evidence, and the pursuit of undeniable proof, can far outweigh the overall need for openness toward the Spirit communication that the message so desperately requires in order to be received and understood. Every medium has had someone sit, their entire body locked and defensive and have them say 'prove it'. On their terms, in their time and nothing less than everything they want to hear would satiate them, and even then they may still just put it all down to luck.

Perhaps in part this is to do with the televising and editing of Mediumship. Many of the public watch shows that portray amazing feats of incredibly accurate evidential Mediumship yet do not realise that what they see may be at most a two hour demonstration edited down to thirty minutes, including advertisement breaks. Perhaps it is just human nature.

Either way there can be no doubt that the modern public view of Mediumship and spirit communication has travelled far beyond the initial packed concert hall days of amazing mediums like Helen Duncan, Estelle Roberts and Emma Hardinge Britten, to name a few. In the past, these pioneers of Spiritual communication and contact, as well as those in Spirit whom they channelled, were working so very hard to raise the profile and understanding of the methods and nature of Spirit.

In the world today, however, it is commonplace now in every town and city to have a plethora of spiritual practices and psychic services on offer, covering the entire scope of charity nights to psychic suppers and séances. The world has indeed undergone a spiritual revolution and become a more spiritually diverse place. More importantly a greater level of basic awareness has been reached by everyone, but for what purpose and to what ends.

What has been the cost of this upsurge in not only awareness but expectation of the public perception of what it means to receive a Spirit communication? There are times, particularly when we are faced with expectation and scepticism that it seems that we often move further move backwards, rather than forwards in our projection of the message from Spirit.

In our bid to get the word out there and make it all so much more accessible to all, have we somehow lost our spiritual way in the physical world. Worse yet, how many actually understand just what the end-point of Mediumship, and of being a Medium, truly is?

What is the Point?

The mediums goal should always be to accurately identify any communicator and relay, where at all possible, evidence of the past and present to the sitter. If for no other reason than as a means of identifying and eliminating any doubt that the correct message is indeed going to the correct person, particularly of the spirit communicator does not present themselves as looking for any one individual. This then gives everyone present the opportunity to recognise or eliminate the spirit communicator and the message to follow as being intended for them. In addition the process of giving evidence also presents an opportunity for the medium to identify with the energy of everyone present, particularly those who claim to be able to understand part of all of the information being brought forward.

However, it may come as a surprise to note that not everyone who attends a spiritualist service or a demonstration actually wants to be involved in the process of receiving a spirit contact. Many are there to support others, or out of curiosity. On the opposite side of the scale there are those who desperately want to receive a message and will attempt to accept any grain of truth or relevance with gusto. Everyone else falls somewhere between these two categories and it is the responsibility of the medium to identify with the intended recipient and to be able to place the eventual message where it needs to be delivered.

Accurately placing the correct communicator with the correct recipient is the key to success in any given message. While many of us lead similar lives, we do all have unique qualities and memories, and it is these that the medium seeks to uncover from their communicator.

To do this, the medium must be aware of the connection not only between themselves and their contact, but also the connection between their contact and the receiver as it is channelled through. When you have a potential recipient that is not the actual person to whom the message is supposed to be directed the link feels different and does not quite flow correctly. This is partly due to the communicator not recognising the potential sitter, leading to a disruption of the even flow of energy in all directions which provides a very different sensation to that when you have the communicator and sitter correctly matched.

Experience and practice is the only way to familiarise oneself with this and again relates to the need for continued work not only on ones' own self and development, but on our ability to work with and strengthen our link to Spirit at all times. Eventually, you can be able to know the difference between a right and wrong potential link within a matter of moments. When this occurs, just apologies and with respect and good intention for any error you may have made, simply move on to find the correct recipient. They are there waiting, you just have to keep questioning the communicator for more information in order to find the key that will eventually open up your recipient to the presence and identity of the spirit contact you have. That is, of course, provided that the recipient is open to the possibility, or wants to be receiving the communication at all.

I remember giving a church service one night and this very strong communication came through from a gentleman who wanted to talk to a lady in the audience about a young child that had been born here on the earth plane and was now at early school age. On this occasion the gentleman presented himself in my mind directly beside the lady he wanted to speak to. This was, for me, a very rare occurrence to actually see them standing beside their recipient so I asked her about him and she informed me that she did not know who I was referring to.

I took this back to the gentleman and his manner and attitude was adamant about who he wanted to speak to. Not wanting to pursue the issue I queried him a little more and he said very little other than giving out names and some evidence which I opened to the entire congregation. All this time he was standing beside this lady. No-one else could understand and I once again, becoming more than a little desperate now, returned to her and asked once more if she could understand any link to this contact. Again she declined, this time with a shake of her head. Apologising to the congregation and to the gentleman in spirit, I asked my guides to move him back and bring forward someone else. Talk about an awkward moment; I was thoroughly confused because the link and connection when I spoke to her had felt so right and so in place.

I continued with the service, more than a little off my stride but found my feet again with more well-placed links and some very detailed evidence and wonderful messages of love and support.

Unbeknown to this lady, my wife was in the congregation and was placed sitting directly in front of her. You can imagine my surprise at the end of the service when, as we sat having a cup of tea, my head still caught up in the link that could not be placed, my wife informed me that the lady had turned to her friend and whispered "I didn't want that man through to speak to me, he went to prison". I have to admit, I was a little taken aback myself because up until that point, it had never really occurred to me that people attending a service may not want to receive a communication.

I can only think that Spirit must have taken pity on me and given me some extra support that evening after that misplaced link to keep my energy going and to give me such wonderful communicators through after that.

What Spirit ask of you

Difficult communication or negative events serve as a good lesson in learning to know not only when your link feels correct and accurate, but also when it is time to stop. That particular evening where the lady refused to take a link that was for her I could have pursued the issue further but something stopped me from doing so. It was my own good sense that this was just not going to work and in deciding to step away from that particular link, and being respectful of all concerned, no harm was done.

Now, when I address a service or demonstration and the Chairperson reminds everyone to answer in a loud clear voice if the medium comes to them, I always add in that if I do go to them and they do not want to either receive a message or speak to the spirit communicator being brought through then please do speak up and say so, no offense will be taken and it is all right to do that. Trust me it is a lot less stressful than the alternative.

Ultimately, the Medium has a responsibility to serve Spirit by identifying the communicator to the recipient via evidential means and to interpret and deliver whatever message they are asked to. That is all the Spirit as asking of you.

Any medium who does this with honesty, integrity, and respect to the best of their ability is giving all that they can.

The medium must remember that they have no control over the conscious ability of the receiver to either understand or accept the information from Spirit. This awareness level and comprehension is entirely up to the sitter or receiver, and their own ability to be aware of the miracle of communication and the wonderful gift from their loved ones that is being presented to them.

Until that occurs, all we as mediums can do, is all that is asked of us, to deliver the message to the best of our ability and to trust in and be aware of Spirit.

Awareness of Spirit

You do not have to be a fully trained medium to communicate with your loved ones in Spirit, all it ever truly takes is a single thought. When we gather our thoughts and send them out to Spirit with the positive and loving intent to be heard, we are immediately linking to those who have passed beyond this earthly life through our focus and connection to them.

There are many times, when working with a Spirit communicator that I have been asked to mention to their loved ones that they have heard the thoughts that have been sent out to them. Often this is received not only as evidence of the continued existence of our human soul, but is also a wonderfully uplifting message back from those who have passed into the realm of spirit back to their family. To know that our loved ones and friends can and do hear all that we send out to them, and that they respond in their own way can bring so much comfort in our times of need. But especially when the good advice and counsel that we received from these individuals in this life is no longer there to guide us as they once did. That is at least not in a way that we may currently understand or even be aware of.

All our family, friends and workers in Spirit do try their utmost to communicate with us, sometimes even more so than we do with them. All we have to do is to open our hearts and minds and to look at the incredible evidence around us that can and does take place. Not occasionally or at times of extreme moments, but in every day of our lives. Even the smallest of details and events may well be a communication from those in Spirit. We just have to look beyond the human need and ego that labels these wonderful events and occurrences as coincidence, happenstance, and just plain luck.

I was giving a private sitting to this wonderful elderly lady one day and can vividly remember that as soon as she sat down in front of me, her husband drew in from Spirit and immediately began to hum a song in my ear. It was not a relatively recent song but it did keep on playing over and over in this gentleman's energy. At the time, intent on delivering the information he was giving, I initially dismissed it as perhaps a part of myself that was getting in the way and continued with the sitting.

The gentleman continued with his communication, his manner delivering his thoughts simply and directly and provided not only good evidence and words of comfort but also events and items from the past, present and some lovely memories they had shared. Yet every time I stopped speaking, this song again was given to me until, at the end of the sitting, I asked the lady if she know of any relevance to this particular song as it seemed to be coming up again and again and again.

She immediately roared and burst into fits of laughter and declared that for the last three days she had been unable to get away from that particular 'tune' as she put it. It was almost as though it were following her wherever she went. I could see the spirit gentleman as he slyly winked at me and said "I had some hand in that" and I again put this to her. She just smiled at me with a knowing look in her eye.

"You know, now you have said it, that makes sense" she told me "he used to hum that song all the time, but especially when he worked about the house repairing things"

To this lady, the evidence that her husband was still around and in her life enough to be aware of this song that was following her around was wonderful news, never mind the possibility that he may somehow have engineered it all. The message that he 'had a hand in it' reminded her of his hands-on approach to everything he fixed in the house and that evening when the sitting was finished and she left I was sure I could hear her offering up a few thoughts to her husband. I have no doubts in my mind at all that he would find many more ways to communicate with her.

Be Spiritual in this life

Although the Spirit world and all those within it will want to aid and assist us whenever they can, not everything that occurs within our lives can be attributed to their actions or their intervention. It is very important that we always remain firmly grounded within our acceptance of what is and is not interaction with Spirit and do not fly off into realms of fantasy or delusion at every small coincidence or occurrence that takes place in our life.

Spirit will work to help us grow and progress both in the physical and in the spiritual sense of things. Where possible they work to help us to heal, to help to open doors and paths of progress. But we have to be the ones to make the choice to not only to step through and accept these options, but to also remain responsible for seeing these events through to completion.

We cannot conceivably presume to deliver up our entire lives to Spirit and expect to make either progress or be able to affect change in our lives in any way. Our loved ones and helpers in Spirit do not want to take over and run our lives for us, for that is detrimental to our benefit in the long run and contrary to our reason for coming here to experience and learn from an earthly life.

While Spirit may work to ease our suffering and to aid us where they can, this is our life and our responsibility to take it forward. Were Spirit to interfere completely with all aspects of our daily life then we would learn nothing from this particular journey. We would become less capable than when we first started this personal journey and quest for knowledge, experience and education.

Our spiritual life and development must therefore work in tandem with our physical development in order to avoid imbalance and lack of grounded thoughts and actions in this existence. Many wise and highly developed individuals have known this throughout the years and entire volumes have been written on the need to live a balanced and fully equal physical, mental and spiritual existence.

One of the best ways to achieve this is through practice and integration of all aspects of our development in equal measure. We should never neglect any one in favour of another otherwise we create a body, mind or spirit that is weaker in one aspect than another. This does not mean to say that we should all strive to be Olympic level athletes with highly developed Mediumship ability and the minds of Geniuses, but we should at least try to keep our lives in a balanced state of being in order to get the best from ourselves at all times.

Work continually for Spirit and respect not only all those whom you serve, but remember to respect yourself and your human needs and requirements as well as your spiritual ones. Avoid if you can labelling yourself as one thing or another and strive to simply be your true self in every endeavour.

You will know when you are at once balanced, grounded and focused on the work that is at hand. All that you do will seem easier, in alignment with your purpose, and the doors before you will readily open to permit you progress to the future. Likewise you will also know when you have taken the occasional wrong turn on your path as events and places will seem out of sorts and not in keeping with what you truly require deep down in your soul.

Take courage in your own abilities, look to yourself and the

Spirit within to determine what you know to be both right and wrong on your own personal journey. Then, completely trusting in all that you have learned, take the next step forward without hesitation. For in doing so, you know that you never really walk alone and that Spirit is always with you on this journey through life.

There are times when understanding such a simple truth as this takes not only great personal conviction and courage, but also faith in yourself and the purpose you have found within the paths and roads that you have chosen to travel.

Never doubt that you are capable to deal with what you receive in this life, for Spirit will always ensure that you are only ever given what you can deal with. This may not necessarily be easy, but will be fundamental to your growth.

Be strong, never doubt and trust that you know in your heart that your own spiritual faith and focus keeps alive all your connections to those around you in spirit at all times.

Chapter 6

FINDING YOUR SPIRITUAL FAITH

Defining Faith

THE CAMBRIDGE ONLINE DICTIONARY defines 'Faith' as 'great trust or confidence in something or someone', 'a particular religion' and also 'strong belief in God or a particular religion'.

In reading these descriptions, the first thing that you will notice is that they are short, concise and to the point. This is, in my particular opinion, an ideal description of the very soul of exactly what faith, and belief, should be. When it comes right down to what we do and do not choose to believe then it is vitally important that we keep it as simple and straightforward as we can. To do the opposite leads to ambiguity and confusion with regard to who and what we believe, and also the capabilities and the limits of that belief within the confines of our human life.

What is it that makes us seek and turn to a belief system? Oftentimes we find that faith is a road that is travelled when all else we are able to deal with has somehow failed us and there seems to be no end in sight or potential for positive movement forward. For many Faith comes only when they reach a crisis point in their lives and have lost both the direction and capacity for knowing what to do or where to turn next.

Sometimes this is a road of personal crisis, other times it

involves the life of another to whom we have a strong bond. We have all, I am sure, at one time asked either our chosen God, Goddess or any number of the world's deities for help or for intervention with a current situation. Perhaps this concerned changes within our position in life, problems with our health, or the safety and security of our family and friends, but always we need it most and turn toward it when any of these or similar factors are in the forefront of our daily life.

There are times when our thoughts and prayers appear to be answered. A friend recovers from an illness, our loved ones are found and returned to us, or a situation clears up and remedies itself. At times like these, faith is all too easy, but can also be very fleeting and forgotten if we let it be so.

Yet there are also times when, despite all of our prayers, and despite all of our wishes and desires, a situation cannot be changed and we are required to face moments of great loss, pain and emotional distress and grief at the situations around us. At these moments in our life, our faith and belief in everything that we hoped to understand can be shaken down to its very roots. Yet these are indeed the moments, during the trials and upset that come into our life from time to time, that our faith is needed more than ever.

In what our human self sees as a perfect world there would be no losses to endure, no pain to be suffered, and no need for poverty or hardship. All would come easy and the world would be filled aplenty with abundance. No-one would need to face some of the horrors that we see every other day of our lives.

Yet, Faith should not merely be a tool for the sorting out of problems or for the removal of obstacles from our life. Our faith should be, and is, an integral part of who we are and in everything that we do. Rather than a few select moments where we feel the need to cry out to a greater power with more influence to aid us, we should instead be making our own faith work for us every day.

In paying attention to our own spiritual practice, and by integrating this into our lives we come to find our faith. By keeping our faith strong and being open to the ebb and flow of the spiritual world and the spiritual aspect of ourselves, we gain further insight into the events that change and shape our lives. We learn to look at them not only from the mundane and human view, but through the eyes of the Spirit that we truly are and so gain a sense of perspective and importance that is in spiritual parallel to what we may have first thought or perceived. In listening to our spirit within, we become able to adapt and grow through even the most difficult of changes by recognising the lessons learned within the experiences we face.

We are here in this life to learn and experience both the joy and pain of living. It is impossible to know the truth of one without first experiencing the nature of the other. Every aspect of the world around us is possessed of a dual quality. In the east, there is the quality of Yin/Yang nature where light and dark co-mingle and exist both simultaneously and symbiotically. Without one, the other has no comparison and therefore no basis for existence in itself. How can we truly know love or understand loss without first experiencing the extreme of the opposite end of the emotional spectrum.

The human part of us cries out for those that we have temporarily lost to the realm of Spirit. It is perhaps one of the most difficult pains that we ever have to endure. Yet, it is only through having experienced the joy of knowing and living a life with that individual that we have come to grieve for the loss. Our pain is not for them, but for ourselves. The real task is to remember that the moments we have are fleeting at best and to cherish each and every one, to live each day as if it were our last and to embrace the gift of this life to the fullest in all aspects.

A key part of this is to never give up the quest for understanding of our Spiritual nature, and to try and never lose the faith that we have, not just in our self, but in the existence of a continued existence of our very essence.

Spiritual faith is not about deferring all ones problems to a greater power or to seek forgiveness for your acts. This is merely a manifestation of our human need to be released from all that we do.

To challenge your own Spiritual faith is to look at yourself in a true light, to find and locate that spiritual source and centre within you, then to nurture and develop the wonderful loving light that resides in us all. You do not need to possess money, to own buildings, or have any excess power or prestige in this life to follow a spiritual pathway. All you need to do is to be aware that the light of heaven, the source and creator of all life, and your own spiritual centre lies within you and you alone. That is the very place to start and where you must build your own place of worship and understanding of your Spirit.

Spiritual Communion

Without any reference to religious practice, Communion signifies a joining of two energies within any single moment. It represents an instant in time where thoughts, feelings and emotions have stopped being separate and indistinct entities and can be, briefly, reunited.

Within the Spiritualist faith, this is referenced in terms of 'The Communion of Spirit' to mean exactly that, a moment where the loved ones we once knew in this life can once again reach out and be known to us. It is the fundamental aspect of any mediumistic communication.

Although the Spiritualist faith has seven principles and guidelines to remind us of our movement and direction in this spiritual journey, I often consider this to be a key principle within the ideal and faith that lies at the heart of Spiritualism. This identifies with the fact that we, as spiritual beings within a human body, can be part of a greater act of sharing and unity. This is a divine gift that permits us to connect with not only those who have gone before us in this life but also directly to the divine power that flows and forms the very essence of all that is.

This act of communion intimates a relationship that is shared directly between ourselves, the world and situations that we are currently living within and those in Spirit with whom we the act of communion occurs. In understanding this principle, we become aware of the fact this this is a link not only to Spirit, but that it must also connect into the Spirit within ourselves.

Through realising our own true nature we can then see that the communion is a truly divine occurrence created through a directed and intentional act of divine expression and absolute universal love. We are not only of Spirit, but are Spirit and so we are able to bring forth and provide evidence of the continual existence of the Soul to those who need it most.

Our Spirit Link

It is through our own natural connection to Spirit that we are once again able to sense and experience that vital and everlasting essence of those who have left the physical realm. This may be the Spirit of our loved ones who have passed before us and who watch over us, or perhaps our past friends and acquaintances who simply want to be remembered. It may even be one of the many teachers from within the realm of Spirit who have knowledge they wish to send forward that is of benefit to us all.

Our spiritual connection permits all that are still here in this earth realm to once again engage directly with those that have passed into the realm of Spirit. It is through our own spirit and understanding of self, and this divine connection and communion to the Spirit of those around us that we open pathways to an inner healing that we often never knew was ever needed.

When this healing is permitted to occurs, the importance of the true definition of communion, through this divine acknowledgement of continual existence, comes into perspective.

The act of communion itself indicates a shared occurrence or experience of two-way communication, and not simply a one-way expression. Throughout any Mediumship message, such as the communion between Spirit and recipient occurs and communication develops, the recipient should feel and know beyond any reasonable doubt that the true essential essence of that loved one is there. It is only then that the essence and expression of divine love from one spirit to another truly takes place.

It is no coincidence that when we are truly at our lowest, or when tides turn against us, that those in Spirit can and do work directly to be with us to offer support and love in whatever way they can, or we are able to perceive. The greater our suffering, the more they will ensure that they are likewise able to communicate their desire for our wellbeing. Being of Spirit ourselves, we are never truly separated from those who have passed from this life back into Spirit. Just like when we shared a physical life with them, their love and concern for our wellbeing is still strong and they will help us whenever they are able.

Any who develops themselves along the path of Mediumship must understand and use this gift of communion as it was meant to be expressed: completely and utterly from the essence of divine and eternal love and for the benefit of mankind.

Spirit never speak idly or for little purpose, but in order to fully understand and realise all that they have to teach and give, one must be open to the possibilities of communication in the first instance. To do this we should always seek to understand more of ourselves and the realm of spirit, in doing so the eyes and mind can be opened to the evidence presented and our spiritual connection and faith will build upon itself.

Building your Faith

Only you can truly decide on what to accept or disallow within either your life or your own personal spiritual journey through this existence. Many along the way will certainly offer you guidance and assistance but only you will know what is truly the correct path and choice for you.

Regardless of your choice, be it Spiritualist, Christian, Hindu, Buddhist or Muslin, it is purely a personal journey and one that you must take ultimately on your own. Be aware that any doubts, fears, misgivings or worries that you have will be brought forward by the human ego and not from within your eternal Spirit. Ultimately, we are all treading the same pathway. We just happen to take some alternative routes around each other in order to get there and none of us in this life truly have all the answers.

Practice Patience

When I sit in circles or meditation groups, one of the biggest barriers to progress that I see for many who are in development is a lack of patience, not only with themselves, but also with their perception of the Spirit realm and how they think it should work.

As I mentioned earlier when talking about the mechanics of Mediumship, there is both a process to follow, and progress to be made before we can honestly see results that can allow us to apply our experiences to any part of our lives, and not just the spiritual.

I am sure we all have mental scars from when we first tried to do things in our lives. Even something as simple as learning to ride a bicycle, unassisted and on our own, will have resulted in situations that taught us tough lessons and moments of doubt and joy. Personally, I think I went through a full pack of knee and elbow plasters and a lot of tears before I finally got my balance right and steered my very first 'real' bicycle away on my own. It took great courage and a learning to pick oneself up, dust oneself down and carry on despite the fear. But what a feeling when it happened!

We all want to experience that feeling of success, to relive those moments such as when we conquered our ability to ride a bike for the first time and feel the wind in our hair, and the elation from getting something right. It is only natural to do so, and to want this for ourselves, for it shows that we are ever learning, ever growing, and still capable of moving forward through life by learning something new.

Yet it is often our desire to succeed at all we do that proves to be the biggest barrier to our completion, and sometimes this drive to excel is the very thing that prevents us from progressing along our Spiritual journey at all.

We must all learn to be patient and slowly build skill upon skill, and in finding our faith in spirit there is no short-cut and no easy route, it is just like learning to ride a bicycle.

In order to build our faith we need to first experience the means, methods and experiences that will set us on the path toward our first realisation of truth. We must always seek to balance out the way forward between the human need for success, and the spiritual requirement for understanding and control of both our own self and the forces at play around us.

Having our eyes firmly fixed on what we perceive to be the ultimate end-point of our efforts often brings with it nothing but a slowing down of our own development and progression.

When we are looking so far across the horizon that we fail to see all the events around us we sometimes do not acknowledge at all when we leave the path we thought we were travelling and begin to drift away from our true purpose. When we become so fixed on the end of the journey, how can we hope to safely navigate the most appropriate route for our own needs, instead we just cut across in a straight line, oblivious to where our feet take there next step, and to what lies immediate in front of our path. Yet, it is also so very simple to prevent this by staying true to the route and the journey and taking the time to find the way forward that best suits us..

To avoid falling prey to all our own pitfalls and problems that we will inevitably throw into our journey, we must learn patience. All steps taken along our progression should be evaluated and then learned from. We should become familiar with the power of Spirit and the responsibilities that are given to us in the moment right now, and not go looking for more and more before we are ready.

Jumping forward beyond the reach of your guides and helpers, those in the physical world as well as the spiritual, and not being aware of or listening to the help they want to give merely means that you will be required to backtrack at some time in the future in order to catch your breath and focus once again.

Building our faith requires putting trust in Spirit, those who work on their behalf, and in ourselves. Until we can be in a place to deliver that trust into the hands of another and accept their aid, progress will be difficult. We all need to learn to trust and in turn to receive the gift of compassion and assistance from those around us, in permitting others to share our lives, we are already well on the way to building faith in those around us and the hands and spirits that guide us all.

Your Reasons Matter

I often tell people when they ask me how I became a worker for Spirit that it all started with a small child who had empathy for others pain, suffering, and who wanted to help. This was not an abstract term for myself but was in fact a simple truth. For as long as I can remember I would want to be of aid, to be of service and to be of use. This created in me certain attributes that were of value and of worth, not just to me but to the spirit workers around me.

What I failed to realise though, is that this was also a barrier to my progress. Not initially, but as the years rolled on I had become dependent upon my need to help others, particularly my family, almost to the detriment of myself and those around me. At a moment's notice I would dash out of the house, sometimes inadvertently and inappropriately, to rush to the aid of my parents or a colleague. I would make promises to help others, and then afterward would often blame and mentally punish myself if I were unable to do as I had said or hoped that I would.

How could something so positive and helpful have become so detrimental and harmful?

The answer lay in the part of me that found a sense of worth in putting everyone else first; the answer lay in the ego and what it obtained from the acts of helping others.

This, I can clearly say from experience, was anything but a

healthy relationship to have with one's own self and is anything but an acceptable way to live one's life. I may have had my faith and belief in Spirit, but where was my belief within myself being founded that I needed to serve others so completely. Did I have so little appreciation for my own Spirit?

The answer when it eventually came to me was a resounding 'Yes!'

Fortunately, with the aid of others and a resolute need to change what I had become aware of the cycle was broken in time. I have my wonderful wife to thank for eventually opening my eyes to the facts. However even with her help and patience, this still took a tremendous amount of personal time, resolve, and discipline to mend fully.

Once I had learned to let go of this, my own development flourished. Ironically my outdated beliefs in what I was and what I should do had been the very lynchpin that was holding me back from knowing myself. After I had acknowledged and come to terms with this, getting to know Spirit became a lot easier.

Understanding and openness with regard to our own perceptions is the key to clearing out all that you do and do not need in your life. To finally rid ones self of many of the issues that we carry with us throughout our live is also perhaps one of the most difficult lessons to learn but one that is entirely fundamental to our progression in any and all aspects of whatever we wish to accomplish.

Learning to release comes through examining and honestly appraising what you believe to be true in every endeavour that you undertake. Always work from a point of positive growth to polish up the soul's mirror and take a good, long hard look at what you truly need in order to sustain you in all aspects of your being.

Start any form of self development or spiritual awareness by being honest with yourself and work as hard as you can to shake off any baggage that you carry. There are many techniques for this from visualisations to meditations and more. See what works best for you then tke the time you need to ensure that this is applied to whatever it is that is holding you back, dragging you down, or occupying your thoughts.

Always remember that Spirit always support you in every attempt to succeed and they love nothing more than to see you take another victory step forward in your goal to know yourself, and to know them. The more you work on yourself, the greater they will also work with you to realise your goals. Just trust not only in Spirit, but also in yourself and work toward finding some faith and hope for all that you may achieve.

Beyond Faith

I have mentioned before that, when the combined power of your own Spirit and those who help you from the spirit realm work with you then there is no limit to the progress you will make on any Spiritual journey. Throughout the years, there have been hundreds if not thousands of dedicated workers for Spirit who sought to do little else than simply spread not just the word, but the truth of the miracle of communication and the existence of the soul beyond physical death. These were people who clearly did not only believe in the power of Spirit and the spirit realm, but whom deep down in their heart knew that all they had seen and experienced was in fact a universal truth.

One of the most incredible after-effects of achieving spirit communication and receiving a message from a loved one is that it has the capacity to take your belief, and expand it beyond this human need into the spiritual part of you. This is the part that stops believing, and start knowing the wonder of the Spirit that we all are deep down inside.

Begin this process by finding faith in yourself and know that you can cope with and overcome all the obstacles that keep you from your goals in life. After this, finding faith in the Spirit world suddenly does not seem so difficult or daunting, because deep down in your Spirit, that faith has always been with you and will never leave.

Be open to all Spirit

The more we become familiar with Spirit, and the methods in which they work then the easier that this awareness and knowing will flow.

I have always felt privileged to work for Spirit and to achieve the sense of knowing that our loved ones are always around us. Whenever I have those brief moments of faltering or hesitation then Spirit always finds a way to gently tap me on the shoulder and let me know they are around.

I was once travelling to the far north of Scotland to give sittings and a service to a local church away up there. All the private sitting went well, but for some reason I felt very nervous about the evening service. Perhaps it was the five hundred mile round trip or the lack of sleep the night before but I just felt on edge.

There is a song that I usually play on my way to any church where I give a service; it is a beautiful piece of music by Howard Shore and Annie Lennox from 'The Lord of the Rings' movie soundtrack called 'Into the West'. I had always felt it would be a lovely piece of contemplation as it details about how our souls always go home to where they truly belong, but never fully leave us forever and we will once again meet in another place. On this particular evening I did not have it with me so I hummed and sang it to myself throughout the day.

That evening, during the service, 'Into the West' was played as the contemplation music before I gave my demonstration of Mediumship. I can tell you that I was beaming with delight all the way through this incredibly moving and very personal piece of music. I knew that Spirit was just saying 'Calm down, see, everything's normal and as it should be'.

After the service I spoke to the lady who prepared the music and told her this story. She informed me that she had not even heard it before until that very afternoon before I was on my way to the service. She had planned on playing something else that night and had actually stumbled on to it by accident and there was just something about this particular song and the words and music that made her decide to use it instead.

When we are faced with events like these within our lives, it is so easy to listen to the ego and simply throw them off to the realms of coincidence and chance. But to me, as it is to many workers in Sprit the truth is so evident in front of our eyes, ears, minds and heart that we cannot help but progress from a level of believing to knowing.

All we need to do is get ourselves into the right frame of mind and the right place in our own Spirit to accept the wonderful and miraculous communications that occur every single day of our lives.

Chapter 7

THE RIGHT PLACE

Releasing Negative Thoughts

THERE IS ALWAYS A right place and a wrong place to work from.

Never forget that throughout our life, all our loved ones and friends in Spirit will support everything that we do and for the benefit and betterment of all. It is not enough, however, for you in this life to be focused only on others and we must also work on the one person we often neglect to nurture, ourselves.

First and foremost, we must always be aware that all the work we do for spirit is an aspect of divine love and healing. Sometimes this is not only healing for the recipient but also for the spirit communicator and even us at times. You only have to pay a visit to any spiritualist church or group and there you will doubtless find a healing book or other object in which visitors and members of the congregation can place the names of those they know whom may benefit from the positive and healing thoughts that can be generated during the service.

When you listen to any spiritual prayers or contemplation, the thoughts invoked are never those of pain or suffering. The direction and flow of thoughts but are always designed to raise the vibration and energy in the room to direct our Spirit to send out both positivity and healing towards all those areas in our world where it is needed the most. This is done because all our thoughts have power and potency, and we must always work toward in keeping them in alignment with our true spiritual self. As every thought we process has the power to affect change not only in ourselves, but also in others, we must be aware of how we use our intent and focus at all times.

As human beings, we are ultimately flawed in one respect or another and it important in our spiritual journey that we learn to make peace with this aspect of our character. To lose ones temper, to feel anger or frustration is not in and of itself a malign or adverse act. Often we need to let loose our emotions in a negative way to release and be free from the stresses and emotions of this life and we should feel no shame in doing so. Provided we do not hang on to these negative thoughts and feeling to the point of causing either ourselves or others to suffer.

To potentially generate constant negativity and direct it toward another individual, and to cling to and not release those thoughts does neither ourselves nor others any good in the long term. Permitting a momentary release of negative emotion to clear ourselves of them is entirely different from holding onto intent and focusing negative emotion to fuel more equally negative or adverse actions.

For every thought that we release into the world is, like any other energetic action, it is subject to an equal reaction be they positive or negative in nature. Clinging on to our negative emotions not only cloud our thoughts but also obscure the loving nature of our Spirit and consistently giving out only negativity with intent to wish harm will eventually be returned back to you in one form or another. When you experience negativity, learn to release and leg go in all aspect of how it manifests.

From Positivity

As workers for Spirit, particularly those who choose to develop their thoughts and abilities, it is vital that we learn to release our negativity and give out only good thought leading to good action. Working from a place of internal light to promote love and healing toward all our fellows not only presents us with a positive platform to grow from, but also serves to act as a beacon of positivity to all those in in this life and in Spirit who draw close to us.

No-one truly enjoys living their life with a focus on the negative, but they mind find this more comfortable and stable than the alternative. When faced with the capacity to change, it can be a frightening experience, particularly if we have settled in certain patterns for a long time. The only way to make such change as needed is to trust in oneself and others, and to take small paces forward to seek the place of positivity within, for it does exist in all of to one degree or another. It comes from the loving spiritual light within us all.

If we stop for a moment and reflect in upon ourselves, we will eventually realise that every one of us has not just a thirst, but a deep rooted desire to find only positivity, harmony, knowledge, enlightenment and progress within our lives. This is our acknowledgement of the loving Spirit within and if we allow it to be recognised we will realise that our Spirit does not ever intend to harm or cause pain to others. It desires and seeks only acknowledgement of our true soul's purpose in life, and is all too aware of the risk in holding onto the negative emotions that we sometimes possess.

Certainly our emotions serve us well in our lives, but we must never become a victim of our own shortcomings and emotional issues that are representative of our physical environment and restrictions. As a medium we must always be cognizant of the emotions of others without being adversely affected by them. Compassion for others is necessary in order to be aware of the need sand requirement of those around us, but there is a fine line between compassionate thinking and sympathetic empathy. Those who are hurting or experiencing pain and discomfort in their life do not need our sympathy, but our compassionate nature in order to help them work their way through the difficulties that they may be experiencing at the time.

To work as a medium, we must always be capable of controlling our responses and of finding that place to work from that is from the position of compassion and healing for those whom we are trying to serve. If we are unable to feel anything for, or relate to, the people we proclaim to want to help then how can we ever hope to be of any real value or service? Likewise, if our good intent is overshadowed by an excess of emotion and we are unable to detach our sympathy from our empathy, then we cannot function appropriately within the role. We become too close to the emotions and issues involved.

Compassion

Like everything else in life, learning to understand and be compassionate for others is not just a skill that can be picked up by wanting it to happen. To understand compassion, one must experience the importance of the power and effect of healing. Anyone who has worked their way through a process of healing, either physical, emotional, mental or spiritual will understand this and all of us have at some time felt the immediate effects of even the most simple words or actions which just seem to make our pain disappear. They may be healing words of heartfelt and sincere apology that takes away our most terrible of emotional pains, or the administering of a plaster and a 'kiss to make it better'. The effects can be very profound and immediate, not because of the action, but because of the intent and loving compassion for healing that is the true power behind them.

Is it not a simple truth that when we work from compassion, our ability to heal both ourselves and others becomes more open and accessible?

If we truly set our minds to it here can be no end to the positivity, light and healing that we can bring into our lives and all those around us.

To be permitted to work with and aid others is a wonderful gift that we can all choose to share with the world and is an opportunity to make both a difference in the lives of everyone that you may come into contact with.

We should never forget that Spirit is always working to present us with the opportunity to learn and progress. Never turn aside the opportunity to learn to further your healing abilities wherever it is presented. Healing is the very core of all that we seek to achieve on our spiritual journey, sometimes it is what we need and others it is what we are required to deliver, and wherever possible we should be working to put it into practice.

Pitfalls of Ego

We all enjoy being given either praise or thanks we all can relate to that good feeling inside when we are recognised for something that we have done well.

As a spiritual worker, however, we must always be aware that there lurks a hidden danger within all efforts to praise. Not from those giving it, but from how we choose to interpret and use the praise that is given.

Regardless of the intent and focus in which praise and recognition is given it is so easy for us, as human beings, to become dependent upon or fixated with how we are perceived. Within these moments of given praise, we must be aware when our Ego begins to rise, as we can often actually lose sight of the Spirit within as the human, physical, need for recognition overcomes just who and what we truly are.

In my youth, I read up on, and was fascinated by, the references to two aspect of our character called 'the self', and 'the Self'. At the time I interpreted these differences as the small 'self' being one aspect of our human nature that craves all the ego and desire that we think we need. The other, the greater 'Self' I interpreted as the less cluttered and more clearly focused aspect that permits us to rise above the baser and ultimately self-destructive need for unnecessary fulfilment. It is finding this balance between 'Self;' and 'Self' that defines much of our motives and desires and which, ultimately, often prevents us from becoming a true Spiritual light in today's world.

Now, in contemplation of all the many years in between, I find that this definition has in no way changed over time. Even despite my understanding and experiences that I have now accrued having outgrown the person I was back then. The essence and source of what drives mu human nature is still unchanged and still relevant to me today. I always try to listen the greater 'Self' over its lesser companion whenever it comes to matters of my Spiritual practices.

Every time that we do our work and we do it well, it is fine to accept both thanks and praise for a job well done, but then it needs to be released and let go back into the world. The very best of our efforts in this spiritual journey should be directed to completing all that we can do as best we can, and then they should be given back to the world of Spirit. That way we acknowledge and release our best of efforts and can move forward unburdened by the past.

We all become aware over the years that it can be difficult to get around all of life's trials without picking up, and sometimes trailing behind us, some personal mental, physical and spiritual baggage on the way. One of the biggest challenges we can ever have is to learn to deal with all those who have told us how good we are and how well we do. For this is the baggage that our small 'self' and our ego loves to delve into and carry well into the future, just to be reminded of how much apparent progress has been made.

In truth, all it does is slow down our progress forward. And may even sets us back further than we can imagine, primarily because those moments to which we cling to are gone. We should learn from them but they are past and our progress lies in an entirely opposite direction.

In order to progress, we must release and step forward. Accept the praise if and when it is delivered and then discard it, for that moment no longer applies and we have shed that moment with every other passing second.

Releasing the ties and aspects of the lesser 'self' does not restrict the true, greater 'Self' and so we can continue to grow and to learn. Even more importantly we will be unburdened and have enough capacity in our lives for new knowledge and experiences after we have put aside that which we no longer require, or which fails to serve us as it should.

Responsible Choices

It is essential, as anyone who follows a spiritual pathway will become aware, that we work hard to understand the concept of Free Will and the requirement of Personal Responsibility as part of our spiritual practices and discipline. For any of us to work in any way with Spirit then these attributes must be developed as fully as all the knowledge and evidence that we build up throughout the work that we do.

It is also vital that we are able to apply this learning and understanding to not only our spiritual development, but also in respect to our understanding of; who and what we are, the routes and paths that we have taken to get here, and the potential ways forward from the place we currently find ourselves. We always have choice and free will, and we are always responsible for our place in the world and our actions. It may not always seem so, particularly when times are difficult, but this is a simple truth that we often fail to recognise.

We are often in places and positions where the impact of the actions put in motion by others brings about situations in our life in which we appear to have no options or choices. This is simply not true in the full sense of the term. There is always a choice and a way forward provided we are willing to accept responsibility for doing so. This is not taking responsibility for the actions or a wrongdoing that may have been inflicted upon is, but it is about taking full responsibility for what to do next. So many of us insist that we must carry into the future moments of suffering from the past, reliving them sometimes daily and to little real gain. Very often we do this because we feel unable to take those initial steps forward from that point by accepting that we have the free will to do so. All it takes is enough self-belief, conviction and courage to assume responsibility for ourselves from this point forward.

I remember a very difficult spirit link I received one evening in a local church in Glasgow. During this link a small boy came through and presented himself to me. The child had been the victim of a violent passing and wanted nothing more than to get a message through to his mother. On this occasion she was not present, but her next door neighbour was.

There are times when Spirit come through and ask that someone be the ambassador for them, usually when this happens it is because they are so very desperate to get a message through to someone in this life who is still hurting so much from the loss of the life they shared. In his instance it was no exception.

Throughout his communication I could feel the young boys desire to help and to give his mother comfort and to try and take away all of her pain. All he wanted to present was memories of times and events where the two of them had shared so many good memories.

Just before the communication ended, he showed me the image of several toys and commented that he still had one with him, that she had put it beside him just before she said goodbye and he had received it and would always keep it with him. He even presented evidence to show that we has around her and her neighbour that very afternoon as they had been talking about him and looking through photographs. All of this was to be made known to his mother so that she would know he was well and never truly far from her side.

The Spirit of this child knew that she was stuck in the events of his passing and could not move forward. All he wanted to do was to try and release her from all the suffering of the past and see her begin rebuilding her life. He closed the communication by saying that he so desperately wanted to see her let go of all the negative emotion that trapped her and to focus on all the memories and positivity that he had mentioned. He so desperately wanted her to do all the things that she had wanted to do and he wanted her to be assured that he would be there to do them with her.

After the service, the lady I had delivered the message to came to see me to thank me for the message and she assured me that she would give it to the boy's mother. After his death her existence had simply unravelled at the seams and she had lost every spark of life that she had once possessed. She told me that all her neighbour did was sit and look through the photographs and talk about what had happened and what could have been. She simply could not look forward to any future without her son and had lost touch with everything that had once mattered to her.

This young child's mother needed to take responsibility to find her purpose in life again and her son knew and wanted to see this happen so strongly that he fought as hard as he could to get that message through. It was many months later when I returned to the church and met the lady I had delivered the message to. She informed me that the boy's mother had taken some steps toward her recovery and had again begun to rebuild her life but still had a long way to go. Although the child did not come back through that evening I know without a shadow of a doubt that he would never stop trying to do all that he could to ensure that his mother was comforted and supported enough to once again find the strength to take charge of her life and to move forward in whatever way she could manage.

Free Will and Choice

Through accepting personal responsibility for wherever we are directed in our lives, we are forced to reflect and to remember that we are, and always have been, the makers of our own future. We have the power to progress our lives in any way we choose, but first we must accept our role within the choices that we made that have brought us to this time and place in our lives.

It is often not what we do with the shadows of the past, but what we choose to do to direct the course of our future that becomes the most important decisions that we make for ourselves.

We always have a free will and the ability to assess and choose what we do with it, so it is important that we keep a clear focus on what we truly need, rather than what we may think we want, in order to make the best informed choice for ourselves.

From this, the very basis of what we need to do to discern between the inherently right and wrong choices can be formed. We associate with these choices in our minds and hearts and so we can begin to form and shape our moral responsibilities. By accepting our moral responsibilities we are better able to then make progress along our own spiritual path, certain in the knowledge that only we can alter or change the essence and direction of our own progress.

Even as external factors influence the events around us, we must always be mindful of the fact that we have a responsibility to take account of the situation and act accordingly, even in the very worst of times.

When incidents occur in which we have little immediate control we must be responsible not only for resolving or attending to the outcome, but also for making the choices to take us beyond this point. This may seem difficult or perhaps even impossible at the time. How then can we hope to deal with situations where we feel completely overwhelmed or unable to act due to the position we find ourselves in?

There is no definite answer to this other than to trust completely in oneself, and trust to our belief and knowledge of Spirit and all those who will draw close to us during our times of need and distress. We have friends and helpers in all aspects of our lives, for every Spirit and soul can easily relate to the suffering of others and, when the compassionate power of love is permitted to shine, it can light and banish the shadows from even the darkest moments in our life. Our inner strength does not come only from and external source of spiritual guidance, but primarily from our faith and belief in the convictions of our eternal Spirit to possess the courage and capacity to cope with all that we are faced with. Be true to this and believe in yourself at all times.

Helping Others

For all of us who are called upon to act as ambassadors for spirit or as aides to those who are suffering or in times of distress, it is this loving light of our own Spirit that gives us the strength and compassion to ensure and support those whom we care for.

For all those who are called onto action in this role it is vital that we take heed of and listen to our internal spirit for guidance for not every action requires that we take charge of and control of the other person suffering.

There are times when what we must do is so much more difficult for all concerned. This may be even include stepping back from certain situations after the initial compassionate work and healing is done in order to allow others to take responsibility for themselves and self-empower the outcome of their own lives from that point forward.

All too often we shoulder the burdens of others for them with the best of intentions, but in doing so we sometimes do little but help them strip away their own responsibility toward themselves. Even under an attitude of kindness, this is ultimately detrimental not only to the being, but the soul of that individual.

Not accepting or adopting the responsibility of others upon ourselves is often one of the most difficult lessons that we can learn. When such times and challenges occur in our life, we must remember that no-one can put right the thoughts, misgivings or actions of another. Likewise, our Spirit will never want us to feel compelled to, for it knows that if we do then we often take away from them more than we could ever have put in place.

It is a wonderful gift to the world when we are there to be able to help each other through the trials of life. Yet we must be aware of the consequences of long term aid and assistance that eventually strips away the responsibility of others for their own well being

In taking on the burdens of others we must be careful not to create a lack of balance in them and replace all our concern and care with a dependency in them.

All of our very thoughts and actions carry with them a weight that defines our world and so we must remain mindful of our focus and the manner in which we conduct and act. By accepting that each of us has both free will and personal responsibility we can be reminded that we are our own centre for control, development and positivity.

When it comes to assistance although we can provide additional support, energy and focus from the thoughts and actions of those around us, we must never forget that ultimately we have the final responsibility to ourselves, for ourselves. To take away that free will and responsibility away from another, will ultimately serve neither you nor them with any degree of success.

Always in your work helping others, do so with the intent to promote healing, rather than control, of the aspect of their live that requires assistance. Doing so ensures that the recipient of your thoughts and actions can assume full responsibility for their lives as best they can once the event has been fully dealt with. Allow them to be empowered by their situation, rather than to become the victim of it and never let them become wholly dependent upon you. Always give them the respect they are due as a spiritual being.

Chapter 8

DOUBTS AND TRIALS

Know you to lessen your journey

IT SEEMS LIKE SUCH a simple concept, to know oneself. We live every day of our lives in this physical existence within the same body and we focus and work through the same mind for our duration here. Yet, beyond all this we also act with the same impulses and reactions that we have learned to put in place through not only one but many other possible lifetime of experience.

How many of us truly know ourselves at all and what we need in every aspect of life. How many of us react, rather, to the desires and notions that we think we should be wanting rather than to the things that we truly need in order to progress, learn and realise our potential within this single physical existence.

It is indeed the rare individual who can stand back and look at where they are going, how they got there, and what comes next without some sense of confusion, uncertainty, or lack of conviction of their place and purpose in society today. Is it any surprise then that before we even get to know ourselves at all and where we have come from, we are encouraged if not expected to begin again and scale for even greater heights. Too often we allow the desire for growth, in any one aspect of our selves, to eclipse and overshadow the need for progress in a more controlled and balanced way. We are always encouraged to play to our strengths and to push the boundaries with them, but when it comes to our weaknesses we can be sadly lacking in desire to look further into and investigate them. Yet it is often in our weaknesses that we find the true potential for growth and development.

For anyone following a spiritual path, regardless of your particular source or focus it is important to be aware of own self and what it truly needs to grow. Very often this involves paying homage to all the efforts and trials that it has taken to get you to any one particular place in life. Before we move on to the next step or the next big event, we need to able to fully absorb and integrate all the lessons that we have thus learned so far. The pace of life in the world today is only as fast and as frantic as we truly allow it to be. Take moments to pause and reflect on all you have learned as often as you can. Only then can you achieve a sense of perspective of where you have come from, and where is the correct place to go to next on your journey.

Personal Reflection

It does you no wrong to hold up that spiritual mirror in front of yourself and just ask a few simple questions of the one we see. Provided we answer truthfully and from a point of positive intent.

These are invariably the very questions that we more often than not prefer to put to others but which can very well be the ones that we are most needing answered within our own lives: "Are you Happy with your choices?", "Do you know what you Need?", "Where is this Going?", "Are you being too hard on Yourself?", "Can you change what needs changing?", "Are you being honest with yourself?", "Are you truly happy?". The list can be infinite and the answers and emotions that come up from putting the truth in front of you may well surprise you.

Whenever we reflect upon and answer any of the questions that arise in our minds, and the resulting answer that we receive is negative in any way we need to stop and analyse why we are choosing to react to our questions in this manner. Although we can all be capable at times of finding it so much easier to be negative in our outlook than to seek the positive, never be afraid to challenge it and ask what it is in particular about that certain issue makes you react in the way you do. Very often is it so important that we challenge our reasons why we are choosing to feel this way in order that we may come face to face with that part of ourselves that is the cause. Only then can we make motion to change.

Our negative side is easy to relate to, it has already delivered the lowest point to you and you need not be afraid of the potential challenges it may face. It cannot be let down any more, or have trust broken any more, or be truly hurt in away way.

In always only acknowledging the negative, you give credence and voice to all your doubts and fears, and there will be no challenge at all for you to overcome. Fear has already won out and you will never need to rise to face the challenge at all. You may feel safer, but you are truly more vulnerable in so many other ways

Strip Away Fears

In order for us to progress, not just spiritually but in any way, we are required to seek ways forward in our lives which do not result in us giving way to our fears.

We can start by seeking ways to become comfortable enough with our own selves, and our own life, that we do not fear to fail. Failure is merely another learning tool, and it is ultimately as much of a positive experience, provided that we keep our perspective open on just what it is we are trying to achieve. Without all the setbacks and failures, as well as the successes and challenges that we overcame, we would not be the people we are today. All we need to be aware of the learning process, and the means to strip away all the fears that we carry.

Often this involves small changes not only in all that we think we need around us, but also the importance that we place on things. When looked at in the true light of perspective, many of the ideals we cling to are ultimately unnecessary. Letting go of all that we do not need or that which no longer serves us is perhaps one of the most difficult and challenging tests we face, but one which brings with it the greatest of rewards.

As human beings we often measure progress through accumulating more as a measure of our success: looking for the bigger house; that better job; the greater salary; etc. etc. etc. Yet, this may not be what we actually need for our Soul and Self to grow and be nourished. These things are only what we perceive we should want to attain and hoard as directed by the current trend of society.

Often what we want and think that we desire is driven not for any genuine gain but more often than not as a replacement for a primal need to control or display our status to others. Ultimately all this does is give us more to fear, more to lose, and therefore can pull us away from our true pathway toward knowing our Spirit and light within.

We should never forget that we are all Spiritual Beings, right here and now, living in a physical life. You are here to learn and grow and adapt and change and to make what you can for yourself, not by becoming overburdened with additional baggage along the way, but by learning to lessen the load until all that remains is our true self within.

How can we possibly come to know and assist others, or reach out a helping hand when we are so preoccupied and busy that we do not have one free with which to help ourselves? How can we show others the way forward when we do not yet know who we truly are, or what it is that defines and shapes our own route and path through this life?

Building Bridges or Making Walls?

Many today are caught up completely in the purely material world and so live and react solely on that basis. As they grow and discover more about the world around them so too grows this need to build a wall around all that they make for themselves. This is not merely a physical barrier, but also a spiritual one that is purely designed to function in and around only their existence and to not actively and completely engage with anything beyond it.

Today, more and more people permit themselves to become isolated within a spiritual prison of their own making until there comes a time when they must face the world outside of the truth that they have built for themselves. When the blinkers come off and the fragile nature of all things physical finally comes to light, they lose both their faith and focus in the world and all they had known and hitherto believed in. They discover that their life has not been about building bridges, but instead has been about making walls that we often do not need.

For anyone working to understand more about their spiritual nature, there is always a wake-up call. Depending upon how much of your own internal baggage you carry, this may well be a very drastic and very difficult experience.

It may come from personal circumstances or illness, it may be from the loss of a friend or loved one, or it may be that it is just time for you to wake up from the situation you are in and to realise that you are not happy with where you are. Either way it may feel like the world around you has just fallen in around itself.

To begin moving forward beyond this point does not necessarily rely upon great courage or an independent resilience to take everything on board. All it requires is that you acknowledge the fears and doubts that you have about yourself and the situation. Then, learn to drop away some of the excess that is holding you fast to the events and issues that are making you unhappy. It need not be all at once and there is no deadline for when you complete the task.

The more you begin to lessen, the easier the act of living can become and slowly you will have the opportunity to overcome your doubts and fears about what you think and feel.

Overcoming Fear

Fear is a learned response that we have picked up over many thousands of years of evolution and psychological development. Some of our fears come from deep seated primal sources and others from events as recent as our parents' and friends reactions to specific triggers and occurrences within life. Fear is very infectious, naturally so as it is a primal survival mechanism, and learning to face and even overcome them is a great challenge for us all.

I still to this day hate touching a flying insect known as a 'daddy long legs' due to my mothers' reaction to them. It is a harmless, long, elongated creature like a large mosquito but has very thin, wiggly long legs that constantly move as it small rapid wings propel it through the air. Generally straight at a source of reflected light, or in my mother's case, usually at her face. That was when the screaming and running away would begin. I can touch one, but to do so literally makes my skin crawl all over, and deep inside my brain a small child is running away from it alongside his mother and a deep learned terror pounds at the inside of my skull wanting to burst out. I realise that this is irrational in every respect, I am a thousand times bigger, heavier and would barely notice crushing it if I chose to do so. However it is not the creature that I am afraid of, rather it is memory of the fear that returns which proves to be the trigger for the reaction. In that moment I empathise with all that had gone before and everything comes rushing back. All rationality is laid low in a moment of fear reaction controlling me and my own choices.

In releasing all the negativity and fear associated with this, and facing the truth of the situation and the cause I can also control it and then overcome my own irrationality.

Not all of our fears should be overcome however, for they act not just as a defence mechanism but also as a safety guard against potentially damaging situations. Provided we can recognise this, all is well and we may function successfully at any of our endeavours. When we begin to grasp and understand the things that we fear, and the causes for them, then we can take the first steps toward releasing ourselves from the hold that our own irrationality has over us. We can act free from fear, but also wise enough to recognise and adapt to genuine issues of concern where change must take place. We gain clarity into what we need.

Many of our fears that we carry and nurture are also tied in to our emotional centre and our own lack of personal belief in ourselves. When we allow this to happen we actually use this very valuable defence system against our own desires and needs. Essentially we become prey to a lesser part of our own self that does not want to face the possibility that we may fail. It is this same part of us that makes us doubt just who we are and what we can truly accomplish.

Doubting Oneself

In many of the development workshops that I have been to over the years I have seen varied different expressions of both doubt and fear that exist within those attending. Often you see occasions where some people are asked to participate and they either refuse or ask to be left out of the proceedings. Many times it is because they doubt that they will be able to do what is asked of them, and so fear the outcome of the self-doubt to the point where it impacts upon and interferes with their actual enjoyment of the experience.

Our greatest tool and weapon against the doubts and fears that we have to overcome is confidence and trust. Every day of our lives we use these two very powerful states of awareness to guide and direct our progress. Oftentimes we are unaware of just how much we do so. Even the most mundane of tasks such as going out of our front door requires a display of confidence and trust, in both ourselves and the environment in which we life. Anyone who had suffered from anxiety or stress issues that has affected them in such a manner will be able to tell you just how important and great a challenge even this can be at times.

It is often the case that we find it easier to have confidence in, and trust, others over and above our own self. So many times we see individuals who just seem to lack the confidence in their own capability to take the next step, but who support fully and do everything that they can to ensure others are able to bridge the gap that they themselves cannot.

Our confidence in what we can and cannot do requires to be nurtured just like any other aspect of our personal makeup and it always must be done by us. Others may help and assist for a period of time but eventually all aid and assistance reaches a point where we are required to take responsibility for moving it on.

Invariably it requires a leap of faith and an acceptance that if you do what you can and what is asked of you to the best of your abilities, then that is always more than enough. It requires that you accept that any outcome you achieve is ultimately a success, for in even trying to do it you have already pushed yourself beyond where you previously stood. It requires that we learn just as equally from our failures and we do from our victories. It requires that you acknowledge that you fear and doubt comes from within and not from any external source, and if you put it aside for just a moment your whole perspective on life may be changed by the outcome of what you are about to do.

It requires that you put just a tiny, insignificant amount of trust in you, and then you take that leap.

Building trust

We can all be very private and personal beings. Trust is not something that just appears in any given moment but which is built up over a period of time. Trust is dependent upon our previous and current experiences and we can let it be built up and reinforced almost as easily as we allow it to be broken and torn down.

Trust can and often does bring with it many opposing emotions, and may require that we give up on our need to be defensive or suspicious in order for it to be effective. To trust is, unlike how many people misinterpret it, not about give over not our control to another or to permit them to have free reign over us. It is about allowing us to experience a moment where we are able to receive assistance from another who wants to help us, as opposed to whoever feels compelled to aid.

Genuine trust should never be given to or put in the hands of another simply as a matter of course or practicality. In order to function, trust must come from that emotional and spiritual bond that we form with all those to whom we know have the confidence and capability to truly work from the same place in our hearts and mind that we do.

When someone asks us to trust in them, we can feel and know when this is right. It will resonate on a spiritual level and we will feel at peace with the decision. Unfortunately, all too often we ignore this in place of the practicality of a situation. At such times, when another individual is not acting in accord with your particular energy or vibration, the outcome will rarely work out well. They may do or say something different and the outcome may not be exactly what you thought it was. You will feel that your trust in that person has been broken, but truly it was never there to begin with. What you feel is that loss of trust in yourself, and your own judgement.

As always, we must work hard to be released from all that we do or have done, for the past brings with it lessons and education only and does not necessarily have to impact upon the future. It is we who bring that with us. Learn, release and move on.

Trust in Spirit

There is no difference between working with another person, and working with Spirit. The link between our own experiences, confidence, trust, doubts and fears remains exactly the same. The only difference is that we must not translate the human qualities and attributes that we pick up in life on to our colleagues, guides and loved ones in Spirit.

Spirit will never work to hurt us, but they will work to challenge us and test us to become something greater than we actually are. Often this means that we will find ourselves in positions and places where we have the opportunity to put into place all that we have learned to date. Embrace these opportunities and never turn your face away from them. Keep in check the human aspects of doubt and fear and just have the faith and trust to take even that small step forward.

If you fall short of your goal, then review and revise what you may have been able to do differently and do not allow your ego to punish you for it. If you achieve any degree of success then know that you have forever changed the course of what you are capable of and push all those doubts and fears even further aside.

I remember the first time I ever took a spiritualist service on my own. It came in as a call from a small church in Glasgow that had just had one of their mediums drop out and I had been recommended by a colleague. I had been there before, working with a fully trained medium so they knew me, knew how I worked and generally what to expect.

I agreed to do it, and as I hung up the telephone felt an immediate urge to literally run a thousand miles in the opposite direction and no amount of haste would have been enough. Literally, the word terror did not quite capture how I felt. I knew that this was momentary however and just let all the initial panic settle down as best it could until only the butterflies in my stomach remained.

I sent my thoughts out to Spirit to thank them for this opportunity and to let them know that I trusted their judgement and would be only too happy to serve. I knew then that they would not let me down and would do what they can to achieve the best communication possible.

All the while, I was aware of the small doubts of my ego trying to creep in and take over to convince me that I was not ready, that I was should be taking more time to practice, that I would not get anything through, that I would look foolish and silly on the platform. It was obvious to me then that this was one of the 'crisis moments' where we can choose to give in to our doubts or we can choose to seize the opportunity.

I took a few moments to reflect upon all that had led me to this point. All the many years spent in personal development and development circles, the time that I had put into it all, the efforts of everyone involved, the sacrifice and the study invested.

I knew that Spirit was with me and that they put this here for one specific purpose. But I still had to choose to accept and take responsibility for my actions and decision. With trust to Spirit in place, and an acknowledgement of all that had come to pass to present this opportunity, I took my first church service.

Value what you do.

That first service was certainly a learning curve, but more from a point of understanding that when you work from the right intention and for the right action then all those in Spirit who want you to succeed will always be there when you need them.

Even today, with my first service well established into my past and safely tucked away into one of the many experiences that I have learned from over the years, there is still a hint of tension and nervousness whenever I take a service.

Any medium will tell you that before they take the platform at any event, the butterflies start jumping around in the gut and the fears and insecurities begin to rise but we all have our ways and means of dealing with these.

For some it is meditation, for others it is prayers, for others it is a walk and a change to clear their mind. No one way is any better or worse than others for each is as individual as the medium themselves. You would expect that as the years go on this feeling lessens and eventually vanishes, but it never does and this is a good thing.

The nerves and the panic that every medium feels rising up before a service show they are still aware of the importance of the work that they do. It shows that they have not become complacent or assuming that they will be able to make connections at a whim and that there is indeed still work to be done.

I always remember to look upon this as a sign that the medium has not yet lost their humility or their desire to serve the spirit world to the best of their ability. They fully recognise and understand the importance and the miracle of this spirit contact and the healing power of love and support that they will be part of. They still respect the power of Spirit and all that it brings in its full entirety.

In seeking to serve Spirit, you must also be ready and willing to be confident about their belief in you. You must never forget the importance of the work and the message that you are part of, regardless of your role and when the opportunity arises, know that your faith and your trust can overcome any doubts and fears you may feel.

PART 3

Serving Spirit

Chapter 9

THE SPIRITUAL CONNECTION

Keeping it Simple

THROUGHOUT OUR OWN PERSONAL spiritual journey we invariably come across many different pathways, disciplines and methods of development to work upon both ourselves and our own capability to serve others.

If we open our eyes to all of the possibilities around us, we will find many teachers and advisors, each one with their own experiences, understanding and philosophy of our world, and the Spirit realm.

It can also be very easy to become overloaded with the myriad of information available to us these days. The onset of the modern era and the ready availability of information through access to various sources via television programmes, online searches, Facebook groups, podcasts, radio shows and more continue to prove to be both a blessing and a curse at times. Simply having access to information and a wide range of source data is by no means a replacement for the actual experience and first-hand knowledge gained from reputable teachers and tutors.

Just simply having access to information on a subject does not ever bring with it the accumulated wisdom and experience that has gone into the understanding of the subject, or the ability to know just how best to use it accordingly.

If knowledge is power the always remember the old adage 'with great power comes great responsibility'. Power that we use frivolously, or without giving due diligence to the outcome of is power lost or misplaced. We should always work with a defined and establish purpose in mind to get the best from ourselves.

As we navigate through our spiritual journey to find our purpose, and our understanding of what it is that we are trying to achieve, we will find many options that appear to be the best methods for doing so. We must be always cautious and aware of the possibility that our quest does not become clouded by the many options and methods available to us.

The purpose of our spiritual journey is not only to learn to progress our knowledge, but also to allow ourselves to release and let go of all the excesses and requirements that our physical, human, self will demand that we need. Very often we simply collect too much along the way from too many sources of information and so begin clouding our understanding of what path in life is best for us. You really can try to do too much, when it is very often about keeping it simple. Yes, being aware and cognizant of other, alternative means of focus, direction and methods of spirituality and development can be beneficial, but not if it begins to affect and overwhelm our original intention in the first place. When we seek to work for Spirit, understanding and utilising the correct methods, and only the correct methods that are suited to our own Self, becomes essential.

Simply gathering more spiritual belief, accoutrements, books and practices does not necessarily mean that you will become a spiritual person who is capable of understanding their own spirituality. We are also human beings and subject to the human frailties. One of these is easily becoming clouded with intent and purpose amidst a sea of opportunity. Stop, take stock of what you want to do and where you want to go and then strip back all else to which you have become attached in your mind to permit you the freedom of vision to reach your goals.

Recognise Your Attachments

I once met a trainee medium during a weekend course on developing our spirituality and improving our connection to Spirit. This lady was someone who had become lost and confused along the way, having picked up far too many other things as she was developing. These were, in and on their own, all perfectly acceptable rituals and affectations. We all possess these as we develop, however instead of replacing one with yet another; these had all piled up on top of each other.

Our tutor that weekend was a very well-known and well respected medium in his own right and one of the first questions that he put to the group that first day was, "What do you do to work with your Mediumship, and with Spirit, and how do you make it work for you".

The group was not overly large that particular day and we all had a chance to answer the question. The final answers were, as you would expect in a mixed group of different ages, genders, and experience levels. When it came round to my turn, the answer was simply "I meditate, find myself, do what I can to let all of that human part of me go, and then send my thoughts and vibration out to meet Spirit and my guides, oh and I throw a prayer out to Spirit as well, just in case!.". I was happy with this and it seemed to tick in some part, at least some of the criteria that the tutor was looking for.

As the answers passed around and it was this lady's turn she began to not only list the items and things that she did, but she also had to count them on her fingers one at a time to make sure they were in order. The list was something like "First I get my meditation cushions ready, then I light seven candles for my seven guides, then I find my balancing crystals and hold these at each energy point to align my chakras, then I get comfortable and put on a guided meditation, then after this has finished ("How long", the Tutor asked, "twenty minutes" she replied) I offer up my prayers to the divine for guidance, then I sit and meditate and I speak to my guides and travel with them, then I ask them to bring forward someone who wishes to work with me".

It was clear from her answer that she had listened to a great many people over the years who had all given her good advice, but rather than making use of what she needed to and letting go of what was no longer needed, she just piled it all together.

This is a very common misconception about working with Spirit, and about being Spiritual. When we are developing our skills, regardless of and no matter what our chosen pathway may be, there comes a time when less is indeed more. Any of this lady's measures and methods may well have worked fine individually, but all together? It merely created this lengthy and complex ritual that ultimately was not about contacting Spirit, but about calming down the human part of herself that demanded all these various means and methods of focus.

Oddly enough, before an hour had passed, this lady got up and left the room and the course without a word. Perhaps she was not ready yet to have her vision of what was needed. I remember watching her leave with a little sadness, hoping that she truly finds whatever she needs to progress and find some peace within her both herself, and in her work.

Too much of a good thing

I have mentioned before that the meaning of this journey is to lose all the baggage, not gather more. Everything that we pick up and learn will serve a purpose for a time, but it is vital that we train to recognise and realise when these items and habits are holding us back in our work.

Yes, our bodies are grounded in the physical realm and will pick up habits, but it is our choice to decide to finally break these habits and to find the simplest and most effective methods that work for us. This is true in everything that we do, from Mediumship to DIY to merely going a walk in the park.

But even in this aspect of releasing and letting go, we must be careful. For it is all too easy to fall prey to our Ego and need for perfection at all times.

I remember a visiting medium who came to my local church who related a cautionary tale on just such a subject that I would like to share. He knew of one of his colleagues who was in truth a very spiritual person and this individual believed wholeheartedly in all that he did. However he was always in the habit of building up on what his definition and personal philosophy of a spiritual person was. His talks, originally once interesting became 'preachy' and identified all the things that we do wrong in our lives, and how we cannot hope to work unless it is from a point of purity. This person stopped eating red meat, because it was not good for his vibrational energy, then weeks later did the same with white meat and eventually fish a few months later. Apparently these were also interfering with his vibrational energy. In the meanwhile he stopped taking alcohol, even on weeks where he had no churches to visit, or places to be. Again, it interfered with his energy. Shortly after, he removed the televisions and radios from his house to negate and 'negative' emissions from the screens and transmitters.

Pretty soon after this out went the microwave, LED clocks, and going to be after 9pm. He drank only freshly distilled and purified water and moved onto only organic, almost raw vegetables to cleanse and purify his aura and insisted on meditating for hours both in the day and evening time.

Now I know that any of us could all do with improving our diet and watching our intake and exposure to some of the more meaningless, but often fun, things in life at times, however there needs to be a limit and a grounding of our journey as we go through it.

It seems to me that this person was attempting to get rid of everything from his life but the one thing they had to, a need to believe that all their ability to communicate was tied in solely to their perceived physical environment. In attempting to drop everything that this person deemed to be harmful to the work with Spirit, they were in fact collecting and hoarding 'losses. Perhaps initially with good intent and belief, but eventually it had deteriorated into an obsession about what working with Spirit is about within their own mind. Perhaps it is this that they need to learn to overcome, but are blinded by the ideal of what they think the need to become a better person. Ideally we are seeking spirituality in this physical life. How can we do that when we fully deny access to this life while on that personal quest for perfection?

Ironically, this individuals functioning in this life was hampered and I remember all too well the closing message of this cautionary tale. This person had created so many conditions and habits that led to the 'right' place for them to be and to work from that it could not be replicated anywhere other than their own home. They had become so dependent upon their limiting needs that they stopped working for Spirit almost altogether.

Live This Life

We cannot ever hope to turn our human existence into a purely spiritual one, for in doing so we miss out on the entire point of this life. We are looking to realise a spiritual existence within a human lifespan, warts and all, through good and bad times.

To turn our short time here into a purely spiritual moment, devoid of all the human conditions and experiences that make us truly who we are seems like such a waste. Life here is for living and for experiencing. It is a precious gift that we give to ourselves in every incarnation that we choose to learn from. To throw it back or reject it by trying to make it what it is not is showing ourselves a great level of disrespect.

We chose to bring our Spirit here in order to learn and grow. This involves dealing with the bad as well as the good, and very often requires that we keep our heads out of the clouds and firmly attached to our physical self and nature in order to do the very best with what we have to hand every day of our lives. To seek to progress, regardless of the challenges and trials we face, and to overcome them in whatever way we can to the best of our ability is to truly acknowledge the strength of the spirit we have within.

If you think that you are doing too much, you probably are. During your journey it is so very vital that you listen to the voice inside you and take a step back, evaluate, then continue on every step, twist and turn of your journey through life. In doing so you allow a moment of reflection and perspective and so are learning to understand not only yourself, but also the world around you in which you must function.

Change and progress do not come overnight and will never be firmly rooted in reality if you do not first take account of what is you truly seek, and the ways to make this happen within the sphere of control that you currently possess.

Influence and Capacity

As is always the truth, the most direct and acceptable routes or methods of reaching our goals lie firmly within the simplest and most common sense of techniques. We must always set out in our understanding with a firm basis for what we wish to achieve at the end of this phase of the journey.

In order to do that, we must be able to honestly and openly take account of where we are now, and where it is that we want to be. If we cannot do this for ourselves, then we need someone else to do it for us. We are all subject to the laws of influence and capacity in ways that we cannot expect to work with or manipulate too far outside of. We are limited by our own sphere of influence, or our capacity to affect that sphere of influence at any given point in time.

To make change in our lives and to reach any end-point of a venture this requires us to look at our overall goal, and then work backwards. This process continues until we recognise and resonate with the thoughts that are generated in our mind or over which we can finally reach some measure of control and responsibility.

As we work through this process we must keep these goals reasonable and well within the boundaries and areas of influence that we are currently able to understand and make use of. No good will ever come from trying to go too far, too fast, without the required discipline or experience required to impact upon and change the situation that we currently find ourselves in.

Work where you are, get where you need to be

I remember once discussing the importance of our area of influence during a church open circle. That evening I talked everyone through the importance of understanding not just what we want, but what we must work at, develop, and often sacrifice in order to get to where we want to be. I can remember at the end of the evening that several of the members came up to me and thanked me for giving them some insight into what they needed to do. In truth all we did that night was open their eyes to the existence of and the possibility of a gap in their influence. It was their own thoughts that did the rest to empower themselves forward and into recognising what they need to do in order to make their goal a more solid reality.

As part of the exercise that evening I told them to imagine that they wanted to manifest a million items, it could be friends, money, houses, hugs, anything that they wanted. They all wrote down their thought and kept it secret. Then I just asked them to stop and think about how possible or impossible that may seem right now at this very moment. Having looked at what they had written most agreed that, unless exceptional circumstances come into play, they cannot at this moment make it happen.

Then I asked the group members to step away from this goal, and to look at what would be the reverse stages along the way. To help I chose one of the most common wishes and problems you hear about today. I worked backwards through the task of making a million pounds. As you can imagine; everyone was suddenly very, very interested.

If we want a million pounds, barring a great deal of luck we will not win it and most of us have no intention of robbing a bank any time soon, so therefore we must acknowledge that it needs be earned through a lot of hard work. No success is ever truly delivered to your door without some requirement on your own part to make it work positively for you. At this point some of them became less interested in the secret of the one million pounds, but were no less attentive to they ways that they could change their lives for the better.

To earn it we must in fact stop looking at the million pound ideal and first realise the way to make it happen, such as via a positive and profitable business venture. Yet, right now we cannot make a business venture appear out of thin air either, simply because there is as yet no concept or plan in place. This is still therefore working outside of the current level of influence available.

The steps before this then is to find the market gap and to work toward understanding the principles of business within whatever it is we choose. Although this is systematic and simple to comprehend, we cannot just make the items for sale appear out of thin air either. This is still far beyond the required level of influence and capability to act upon and there are clearly areas and steps that can be taken to bridge the gap further.

So we continue to apply the principles toward a requirement to learn new skills to manufacture and create. How can we do this when we do not know where to learn the skills? Once again we are working outside of our area of influence, but are clearly getting closer to the problem, for the focus is now away from the goal and onto our own selves.

When we look and search we are able to eventually locate the aid and assistance we need from those who have the requisite skills to teach us and we educate and learn to put into practice the starting point for all that we have thought out beforehand. Then we begin to slowly and methodically work our way back up the list.

Simple, but not necessarily easy, and clearly requiring both time and effort on our part.

So, we have been able locate the place to learn the skills and expend our efforts to do so. From this we are able to introduce the idea of creation and production of the materials to expand into a larger venture until finally we are able to produce on our own. Taking this out into the world we can unveil our product and reach those who require what we have to offer.

The process of learning, refining and creating our own skills as a medium, or as any form of spiritual worker is no different. All we need to do is detach ourselves from the bigger picture, and to find our own level of influence and capability each and every day.

Building your Connection

The methods and logic applied to building our influence and capability are no less pertinent when it comes to working with our own current skill and level of experience as either a medium or spirit worker. We can always be capable of reaching out that little bit more, and to work toward gathering better communication, better spirit link, stronger evidence and reassurance for our sitter. This in turn empowers us with greater capacity for our actions to help and perhaps heal those who receive them.

As was mentioned under the section on 'Mechanics of Mediumship' the link is not simply a one-directional route whereby the medium can stand idly back and wait for Spirit to come to them. It requires much more combined effort to put into place something concrete and worthwhile.

Know your part, Do your part

Above all else, remember that each Spirit contact will work as hard as it can to establish the best link and flow of information possible. You often hear during development groups, particularly in the early stages of someone's development the phrase "Spirit are not talking to me".

This can be a common complaint among trainee mediums, but what they are actually saying is that "I am not able to get anything from Spirit". What is happening is that they do not yet fully understand the mechanics and work required to make that link. It requires more training and more time to be developed in whatever way it can.

Unfortunately the intent and terminology that we use when we talk about ourselves can often be part of the process of what is blocking the contact with Spirit in the first place. Regardless of how much Spirit tries to be able to relay a message, they also require the medium to raise their own vibration and reach out to the information.

Then, they must also be willing to trust in the information that they do receive. This trust must be extended not only to the Spirit communicator, but also to oneself during the process of attempting to communicate.

Failing to recognise a lack of trust, or even perhaps confidence in oneself, can bring forward much of our defensive and reflexive emotions that will try to protect us in whatever way they can. The easiest way to achieve this is by deferring the responsibility for the poor connection or lack of information back onto the communicator, instead of where it needs to be directed.

Trusting in oneself requires not only great courage to implement, but also a great deal of will and control to prevent it from escalating out of control and surrendering every passing thought each moment as coming from Spirit. A medium who gives everything up that enters their mind during a communication as genuine evidence from spirit, when it actually comes from within themselves, will find both their link to spirit and their communicator stalling if not being completely lost and the connection dropping from a mediumistic link to a purely psychic one as they struggle for information.

In surrendering completely any sense of control or responsibility for what is said and done, how can any individual be sure of the actual source of that information, particularly during the elevated vibrational moment made during a spiritual connection?

What to Achieve?

We avoid this by continually working on knowing ourselves, on knowing our part to play in the process, and trying to establish better and stronger links in the work that we do. Sometimes it is done with great success and other times less so. The amount of progress made is ultimately not as important as the act of self-control and learning that goes into each and every attempt to make your connections better for you, your communicator, and your recipient.

Like the dilemma faced in our 'manifesting a million pounds' task, the methods and means are no less simple to understand but not so easy to apply. It takes a lot of work.

If you want to improve on your ability to connect to Spirit, first look at what it is you wish to achieve then work backward until you find the point within your current level of influence that you have control over. Be honest and vigilant in your answers to yourself and will find the way with time and effort.

If the novice, often known as a fledgling, medium wishes to improve their connection it may require them to look at the overall goal and to actually work to understand what they mean by their intent. During a beginners circle in my local church I put this question to the group and many implied that their goal would be 'better connection to Spirit'. When I asked why, it was so they could provide better information to the sitter.

At this point I raised an issue with their thought process. Although their answers sound the same, they are not. 'Better connection with Spirit' is not quite the same as 'better information'.

The connection is what is required for the information to occur, but information comes after the connection, not the other way around. I raised this and asked them to re-evaluate or consolidate what they thought they wanted. Many of them stuck with 'better connection' but this time their answer to my query on why was 'to feel and become more aware of when Spirit are close'. Yes, that was a very good place to start.

That evening we worked our way through the groups level of influence, starting with the goal of 'better connection to Spirit' and working our way backwards through the process of expanding ones aura, taking to guides, opening one's mind, letting the physical drop away, awareness of spirit presence and everything else in between until we were left with an interesting dilemma. Many did not simply know if what they were getting was Spirit, and so doubted the presence and small interactions that they felt. Yet this was also not necessarily wrong, as much of what they were experiencing came not from an outside source, but from within their own body as it adapted and changed during meditation.

Many of the phenomena experienced included sensations over the face, sensations in their chest, heaviness in the legs and many other physical symptoms that were merely aspects of their own meditative state and their own psychic field around them. It became clear the area in which a lot of them needed to begin their improvement was in fact in understanding themselves and their own psychic aura. This is what we worked on.

Recognition of our own clutter and emanations is necessary in order that we can strip it away to find the connection to Spirit. When we took the very concept of connection right back to the level it needed, many found that they were four or five steps away from even needing to work on the connection. First they had some work to do in recognising and letting go of their own body first.

Be responsible for improving

Even now, as a working medium and travelling around to visit various churches and groups to deliver whatever service I can to those assembled. I still use this method to build upon aspects of my work where I would like to improve upon.

Recently, I noticed that although I can readily pick up on emotion, personality and characteristics of Spirit, I rarely got any information on names. I set out to amend this as best as I could. My logic followed through in the following pattern: I Know that Spirit could only work with and communicate through my own experience and understanding; I would like to bring forward more names during my communication; in that case I need to experience more names; being on the lookout for persons names is essential to experiencing them; simply knowing the names is not enough, the communication may not be visual, therefore I need also to hear the names; having found the names I have to make use of them in order to access the sound; therefore I have to work on finding and using people's names at every available moment.

To facilitate this, I began to speak to people by always bringing their name into the conversation. I then noticed that, to many of our friends and family, we sometimes do not use their name every time we speak, particularly if we are looking at them. This was interesting. When I went out to a shop and someone had a name badge, I would use it as they handed me things I bought, "Thank you Jim", "That's great, thanks Sally". Likewise, if someone had an unusual name I would comment on it, ask how it was pronounced, where it came from, who gave them it.

I would query if it was it a name widely used in the family

or was theirs an isolated use. I was particularly investigative of foreign names or some of the more unusual and obscure names from across the country, such as 'Gina, Miriam, Walter, Siobhan, Vincent, Patsy, Melvin, etc. etc.' the list goes on and on. On occasions I event went a walk through cemeteries that I was in passing to see the names etched on the headstones. I sought out anything that involved me actively participating in the search for names and individuals. And before the thought arises I have to say no, no Spirit ever spoke to me in a graveyard, thankfully.

This is still a work in progress, and has been since it I started it several years ago. But I know deep down that Spirit need my experience and my knowledge in order to communicate effectively. The more I grow and learn and experience, the more they can do with this knowledge and the better the communication and link will become.

Don't seek Mediumship, seek Spirituality

Travelling to and experiencing the various churches, groups and events that require your Mediumship services, you invariable meet and come into contact with many people who are not simply curious about Mediumship and the realm of spirit, but who want to know more. I am very often ask you "How do you get to be a Medium", "How can I be a Medium", or my own personal favourite "What happened to you to turn you into a Medium?" Clearly, Hollywood has a great deal to answer for at times.

I advise everyone who asks me these questions, or any alternative, that the best place to go to in order to know more about Spiritualism, the Spirit realm, and what it is like to be a Medium is their local Spiritualist church or centre. Whenever possible I use this as the first point of call, simply because they are the ones who are currently working for and with, Spirit and they will be willing to help you on your journey.

Within any Spiritualist church or centre, there is not only greater potential for development and guidance, but also a wealth of individuals with understanding of the basic driving force behind all intent and act by the world of Spirit and those who come forth to communicate and interact.

Before we attempt to develop any of our skills to any extent, we must begin to acknowledge what working with Spirit is truly about, specifically the healing of others and of ourselves through our contact with the loving and divine nature of the spirit within all of us, including those who have passed beyond this live. This is the true purpose sent through the healing power of Spirit communication and all that it can accomplish. Without the thought to aid or help or heal others to recover from their difficulties and grief, there is no true motive for any Spirit connection to be established.

Chapter 10

Every Healing Thought

Why be a Healer?

THE PRACTICE AND DEVELOPMENT of Spiritualism, and spiritualist thought is not comprised of just one specific practice or discipline.

Although everyone is aware of the more public face of Spiritualism, specifically demonstrations of Mediumship where individuals deliver messages and communication from Spirit, this is merely one individual facet of what Spiritualism has to offer. It is not merely a system of belief but is also a combination of science, philosophy, and religion.

Understanding the methods of working with Spirit is no different to working with any other profession or discipline to be studied throughout the world today. In order to fully understand and work in any field of expertise, there must be a balanced and applied approach to all facets of the core mechanics involved. This involves working through initial thoughts and findings before beginning to study from a fundamental entry level with regard to the core values that lie at the heart of what we are trying to achieve.

This is no different when one is working with Spirit. Although communication provides the proof and existence of continued life, invariably there is a reason for this level of communication, it is rarely undertaken by Spirit just for the sake of it. In most if not all instances it is communication that is brought forward to bring us comfort, to reassure us that our loved ones have not truly left us but are still around and remain a part of our lives albeit in a different way. Above all they still wish to help us heal our loss, grief and sorrow that we carry throughout life.

Spirit works very hard to come to us when we need it most, but never more so when we are in a state of distress. Our loved ones, friends and colleagues, just as in life, do not want to see us suffer in any way and always try to heal whatever issues they can, or give us guidance and direction to aid us in getting away from harmful situations that we struggle with.

It is this healing that lies at the core of Spirit Contact. To understand your capability in working with Spirit, one must therefore be ready to work from a healing basis.

All Healing is Spiritual practice

The art and training of Spiritual Healing is not so different from that of actively being a Medium, it makes use of the same skills, focus and intent to serve that is required for all Spiritual work. Many of the Spiritualist organisations and churches regularly hold training courses and development circles in both Mediumship and Healing. This is certainly the very best place in which to start your journey upon the pathway to the pursuit of Spiritual Healing and understanding of working with Spirit.

There have been some times, when I have been sitting as a member of a development circle and there have been too few members in either or both of the Development and Healing circles to accommodate a full circle that evening. On these occasions the two circles have combined and I have always looked forward to these events, for it gives me a change to flex and develop my healing muscles once again and experience that wonderful and loving connection from Spirit as you are guided in your thoughts and flow of energy to direct that divine and powerful essence to help another.

I have always been drawn to healing and the healing arts for many years. I originated from a martial arts background and have been involved in training and teaching for over thirty-two years. My studies included Judo, Karate and Aikido, which I still teach and practice.

During this time, as you can imagine, you learn to not only defend oneself but also come to learn a myriad of ways in which to cause harm. However with this knowledge also comes the respect for the power and the ability that you have learned. As a result you inadvertently gain both with the discipline and knowledge of how and when to do apply all that you know, if you choose to do so at all.

Whenever you progress within any martial discipline, particularly one so full of philosophy, Zen theory and richness of Spirit (Aikido means 'Way of Spiritual Harmony') you eventually reach a point where you realise that the true meaning and way of study of fighting is not about combat, but peace and a laying down of arms.

It occurred to me that although I know how to defend and, if necessary, hurt, that this was not enough for my true spirit to accept. Before we learn to hurt, it is vital that we should first learn to heal, for causing pain and distress to another is easy. Removing it and helping other, however, shows true strength of character and understanding of the nature and balance of things.

My first real learning experience of the healing arts was in the study of Shiatsu (meaning 'finger pressure'), a form of Japanese therapy similar to Acupuncture in method, but utilising direct manipulation through the skin by the hands and fingers, rather than needles.

In my journey, spanning three years of intense study with a wonderful lady named Elaine who ran a Shiatsu school in Glasgow. There I met and discovered a completely different world to that which I was accustomed, yet part of it was somehow familiar. I realise now that it was the spirit within resonating with the purpose and methods of healing.

Before you hurt, learn to heal

Through the study of Shiatsu, I discovered that many of the martial skills and principles that I had practised for years were so similar to those used to actively remove pain, restore health and promote well-being. There was a definite inter-connectedness to all aspects of the arts, both martial and healing, to which I had previously been unaware. I can vividly remember this giving me a strange feeling of completeness, as though something had come around full circle. It took me some time before I realised that it was my own awareness of my own self, finally coming around to see what it was truly capable of as a more complete being. Of course, I still had a long, long way to go before I would become even nearly accomplished, but that was fine, I was in no rush at all.

It was through this combined and holistic study of living that I had become aware, for the first time, that we all have the power to heal not just ourselves, but others. This ability is part of our own very natural and intuitive state that we all possess. It is only our ego and our need to appear as self-sustaining which prevents us from truly opening our hearts to the soul and spirit of those around us. We see this every day where many choose to take a shorter, easier route to accomplish means and goals that are befitting only their own needs and ends, whereas if they just paused for a moment and opened themselves to the possibilities, they could positively affect the lives of so many more in a much greater way.

A shift in priorities

The world and the attitude of those within it is changing with regard to how we deal with those around us, and the positive and healing contributions that we can make. It is almost as though we are once again beginning to function holistically and as one with the quest to becoming attuned to the true Spirit within. Many of us are realising that the need for commercial, material gain is nothing other than a temporary arrangement attached to their own physical self.

Slowly we are once again realising that this is the realm of our ego and all that it wants to possess, protect and claim for its own needs. But this is not the real people that we see taking action, it is merely the shell and the fragments of associated, self-created desires that we have come to associate with the images of success, victory and survival in this physical life.

Slowly, a paradigm shift in our priorities is occurring as all of humanity is being healed by the same loving and channelled energy from Spirit. For every soul that wakes up to the potential within, and acknowledges the presence of their own eternal spirit, that healing takes place just a fraction more.

We are learning that we no longer need to live in the darkness, surrounded by the fears and insecurities of loss and grief. One by one we are awakening to the miracle and truth of our own Spirit and the incredible power of love and healing that each of us has to offer to this physical life.

We are all Healers

When anyone asks me why they should want to be a healer, I ask them why they deny that they already are. All they need to do is acknowledge that. All of their words and actions have the capacity to hurt or cure at their discretion. If they listen to their true nature and the Spirit within, the course of what is right and wrong becomes unclouded by personal decisions and the true self shines out like a beacon to cut through the darkness that we often surround our own life with.

Why be a healer? The reason is because it is already part of you; you just have to choose to access it.

If you look with an honest heart and mind at the very purpose of healing, you cannot help but understand that it is one of the most important aspects toward a continued life and without it we can never recover from even the smallest of wounds. Regardless of the type or kind of damage that we sustain be it physical, mental, emotional or even spiritual.

No-one ever comes through this life unscathed and we can all benefit from the positive effects of healing, sometimes in ways and for conditions that we were not even aware of ourselves. Even when our time on this Earth is nearing an end, the healing can be such that where it is needed most, perhaps not in the path to recovery, but is in the process of assisting us in the transition back to the spirit world.

It is also not only the recipient who benefits from healing, however. Many who give themselves over to the healing arts do so through a very powerful sense of empathy and compassion toward others. This in turn is nurtured within themselves, making not only their healing more effective, but also allowing them to grow as individuals. In developing our ability to heal, we develop our ability to empathise and understand the issues and problems that many have to overcome. As such, we develop in our own capacity as human beings.

Anyone who has acted in any capacity to help others heal can relate to the change that even the smallest things can do, whether it is a shoulder to cry on, a friend to talk to, or someone more specialised. The act of healing resonates outward from the moment of its inception and can create waves and ripple in a person's life that promotes not only good health but well-being toward themselves and others.

The Healing Thoughts?

In accepting that we are all, naturally, a pure and beautiful healing Spirit within this physical form we can understand why the practice and development of healing within churches and development groups therefore, is vital. Not only in providing a service that many are in need of when they enter through the doorway of any church or group, but also in manifesting love, well-being and positivity throughout the world.

Healing not only serves as a platform for development of the self through understanding and empathy with others, but it gives a great deal back into the world in ways that the healer themselves will not be aware of. It is through healing that we understand what it is to truly care for others, and in turn care for ourselves and all we hold dear.

The study of healing allows us to understand compassion for others and to reach out to offer aid or assistance to those in need. Through compassion we are able to connect to the spirit and source of everyone around us and to gain insight into what it truly means to be human and to have human frailty and weaknesses as well as strength. Through healing we can give hope and betterment to situations that may otherwise be difficult for many to come to terms with, particularly where there is a great change in circumstance or situation around any given issue. Yet more importantly, it gives many a chance to reconnect to another person, spirit, or humanity in general with which they have become unattached. This may be through and means such as mediumship, spiritual healing or direct manipulation such as massage. The means is not as important as the act itself. Very often what many people need is merely that connection once again to the world around them, and the belief and hope that life is not gone but merely changed.

To anyone who wishes to work with Spirit, I always advise that they become familiar with any of the healing arts either as part of, or before undertaking any study into Mediumship.

Learning to feel for others.

From my own experience, learning to heal and to be involved in not only the energy, but the experience of connection to others with the pure intent of helping them to overcome difficulties opened up within me aspects of my own Spirit that assisted greatly in my Mediumship development.

Through learning Shiatsu for healing I discovered that I had inadvertently developed my own awareness of the emotions and flow of energy that leads us toward compassion and sympathy for the human, and spiritual, condition itself.

It is very difficult, in any way, to work Mediumistically without understanding the need for compassion with regard to the issues around both the Spirit communicator, and the recipient of the message. Whenever Spirit comes through, there is always a meaning to the message and they will have a desire and an issue that they are coming forward to help resolve. It is our compassion to understand and relate to the needs of the body and spirit that permits us to tune in to and comprehend the hurt that needs healing. Without this, the true meaning of the message can sometimes be lost or left behind. When a recipient sits down in front of you and you begin to connect to the Spirit within both them, and with the communicator moving in to connect with them it is not our desire to connect that fuels this moment. It is the power of that Spirits love and desire to mend the hurt, or to give aid, that draws them close. By feeling and experiencing the power of compassion in every aspect of the communication, we can gain greater levels of understanding to empower the link we make.

I remember giving a private sitting while visiting a far flung church in the north of Scotland. During the sitting a lovely middle-aged lady and her daughter entered the room and sat down. While they introduced themselves, I began tuning into the connection between them and pushed out my awareness to spirit.

On this particular sitting I learned a great deal once again about trusting to Spirit, for my rational brain wanted to take over, demanding that if a mother and daughter come in for a sitting that statistically there must be a husband/father figure lost somewhere. Fortunately I had long learned that my active brain was not at all what I wanted to engage with during a reading. Instead I tuned my senses into the hurt that was with them both and immediately and older gentleman and lady were presented to me by my guide. Instantly the lady in spirit said "my daughter can't let us go" and then the communication began for real.

Throughout, the pain and hurt being held by this lady and her daughter who cared so much for her slowly became unlocked as her mother and father shared memories, experiences, and even a few in-jokes as they made fun of some of her recent exploits while on holiday. It was an extremely emotional sitting for them. All through it I only wished to see the pain and grief that was evident within the contact, from both the mother and father in Spirit, as well as and their daughter and granddaughter sitting in front of me, to be made easier to bear for this wonderful lady.

I truly hope that she found some sense of release and peace from the sitting, but know that her parents will never be that far away. Not only as they were actively trying to heal the grief and loss she felt, but also because they wanted to see her grow and develop, and heal. Their Spirit and thoughts are with her at all times, even as hers are always with them. Together, I am sure that they will be able to mend the hurt that she was carrying.

It only takes a single thought

All of our thoughts carry power, but especially the positive, selfless ones.

Almost every Spiritualist service will have a moment where they announce and invite the congregation to the existence of a healing book, or other focus for the names of those who would benefit from our healing thoughts. Sometimes music is played or a healing hymn is sung by everyone with which to focus the healing thoughts of all those present. Yet although the methods and style of the healing moment may differ, the focus and direction remains the same. To permit our thoughts to send out love and healing to those who need it, and whose pain is held in the hearts and minds of many of those assembled.

This is the part of the service where our capacity for understanding of compassion and our powers to heal through positive and directed thought is realised. I personally find this a very moving part of any service and, whether I happen to be working on the platform that evening or not. It is where everyone present comes together and join as one, not in the hope of receiving a message, and not in the desire to have our own grief or pain removed, but where we selflessly work for the betterment of others via our healing thoughts.

One of the most amazing aspects of our healing thoughts is the capacity for these to transcend distance and location. When we work together and the light of our individual Spirit combines then in that moment of focus to achieve a common goal we can produce results that can and often do bring about truly wonderful healing energies. In these moments of what is known as Absent, or Distant, healing, there is no real need for those named and focused upon to be actively present. Our healing thoughts and focus are directed not by our physical minds, but by the innate ability of the Spirit within to direct its own loving and healing energies to where it needs to be. All it takes from us is that few moments of selfless thought, yet what a difference we can make to the lives of others by focusing our positive intent to heal out into the world.

Our healing nature

The act and undertaking of Spiritual Healing is not a new discovery for the process and the knowledge of attuning to Spirit to seek aid and assistance in healing another has been around for as long as we have been here manifesting this physical existence. Throughout so many ages and the rise and fall of numerous civilisations, thoughts and prayers to the myriad and varied manifestations of Gods, Spirits, Totems, Foci and the planet itself have all been making use of and activating this most wondrous and miraculous gift of healing. Every culture and religion has tales of individuals of recognised ability who were able to mend the ills of others, to remove pain and suffering and who all tried so very hard to encourage others to look within and see the genuine and loving light that was the reflection of divine love within the mirror of our soul.

These individuals have all possessed the insight to look within and recognise the gift of healing that we all possess, then had the conviction to reach out and share that gift with all around them. Within their life, they have been aware of the universal truth of the everlasting spirit and soul within each of us. They have understood the capacity for us to once again allow that light into our hearts to be channelled and directed into the healing arts.

We have labelled them a thousand different terms within a thousand different languages over a thousand different years, we have known wise persons, Gurus, Masters, Witches, Kohen, Shaman, Priests, Kannushi, Wizards, Imam Khatib, Teachers, Rabbi, Philosophers, Sufis, Daoshi, the list goes on and on. All of these individuals and respected teachers have led lives dedicated to understanding the ebb and flow of the power of prayers, and the need for accepting responsibility toward healing those not only in our own culture, but in all spheres of influence across the world.

We are all of the same human family, with the same source of our Spirit and of our existence; there is no difference between the Spirit of one from a foreign culture to that of our own. We all shine as brightly and as strongly as we allow and, when we seek to discard the human ego and come together under one truth and one realisation, that we are all spiritual beings, there is no end to the power of healing and love that we can create and manifest in this world.

Absent/Distant Healing

The great Spiritualist healer Harry Edwards, one of the most influential and knowledgeable men of his time on the subject made a simple note within the very first few pages of his book 'A Guide to Understanding and Practice of Spiritual Healing'. In it he quoted:

"it can truly be said that Absent healing will become the most potent healing factor for the future"

This is indeed, such a simple and profound statement of accuracy and truth. Undertaking the act of spiritual healing, whether as part of a church or group congregation, whether within a home circle, or whether on ones' own, allows us to enter into a state of being where we can, if our motives are true and with good intent, actively participate in a worldwide healing.

There is no energy wasted during the process of any form of spiritual healing. All that remains is never left to simply dissolve away into nothing, it is always of use. Perhaps it reaches all of those present; perhaps it extends out into the world. We may send it to an individual or an entire nation and all our thoughts may make a mountain of difference, or only a small one. Either way, what truly matters is that it does indeed make a difference.

Throughout my time in visiting and attending spiritualist church services and working with healers and all those who have an interest in or walk a healing path, I have heard so many incredible tales first-hand from those who have undergone a healing process. Although this varies between methods of either Contact Healing or and Absent/Distance Healing process. If you were to compile all the tales and stories from across the world of every experience of healing through the power of divine and spiritual influence, there would be no end to the pages in that compilation. All we need to do is to learn to give up on the prejudices and perceptions that our human existence will impose upon us and just simply be open to trusting that the Spirit within can and always does know how and when to heal and be healed, then trusting also to ourselves permit that love and light to flow to where it is needed the most.

Spiritual Healing, regardless of the means of source, and the true divine love that is the essence of our healing power is a gift to all of us and a genuine manifestation of the various message from Spirit that is always being delivered to us.

The gift and ability to promote positivity and healing through our focus, our thoughts, our words, and the manner in which we live our lives and interact with each other can transcend all manner of physical restriction and boundaries. All we need to do is acknowledge once again the Spirit within, and the compassion and divine love that seeks nothing more than to be realised and set free to heal and help all life and existence.

Chapter 11

MEDIASHIP

Historical Perceptions

THE QUEST FOR FURTHER knowledge of Spirit contact and the truth of what lies beyond the veil of death has always captivated our minds and made us wonder. From what is often referred to as the very first moment of recorded modern spirit contact between the Fox Sisters and the Spirit of a murdered pedlar that took place in Hydesville, America in 1848 to the variety of mediumship and spiritual media we see around us today it is clear that this is still something that we all seek the answer to. Often to find the truth for ourselves we must also find the means and method that resonates most strongly with us as individuals, and it can and often does demand a price be paid for our beliefs and findings.

Throughout the history and development of Spiritualist thought, all those involved have always been watched, judged, scrutinised and perhaps even persecuted at times in their pursuit and understanding of the message that Spirit has been conveying to us. Despite this, the importance of what many have discovered and what it has to offer the world has never truly discouraged any of those brave souls who led the way forward to where we are today. Where we are free and able to choose to seek out and understand our own spiritual pathway for ourselves.

If you look into the development and history of the many spiritual messages and messengers that have been prevalent throughout our history, then you will bear witness to a myriad of tales of personal sacrifice, bravery, and conviction that define the very foundation, purpose and human mettle of which our spirit and soul is forged.

From the most modest of spirit contact known as 'The Hydesville Rapping's' to the developments of the process of communication undertaken by some of the most open-minded, open-hearted and dedicated individuals such as Andrew Jackson Davis, Daniel Dunglas Hume and David Duguid to name a few, this intent has always been that of the questing, curious adventurer. The end result of all their endeavours have always been to heal and restore our connection to the Spirit within and to present this opportunity for understanding to the world.

An awakening world

During this pre-modern period that we lived there seemed to be a change and rapid expansion in the awareness of the Spirit inside all of us. Unlike moments of spiritual growth and development recorded throughout history, the message was no longer being heard only by a few dozen or a select group of individuals, the message came from many and was broadcast across the world.

It is true that in the past Spirit ensured that the delivery of the information and proof of eternal life would come through many of the educated and learned individuals within society at that time. This purpose was two-fold, for it not only ensured that the methods and means of contact with spirit could be understood, but also challenged within the scope of the modern scientific world of the early nineteenth century. At this time the world and the spirit within us all had begun to wake up and effect positive change. Shaking away some of the boundaries and restrictions that humanity had put in place for itself for so long.

The industrial revolution had boomed and the common individual now had, more than ever before within their reach, better means of learning, schooling, support and understanding of the world around them. The bonds of caste and structure were slowly moulding into the future and life that we know today. All aspects of society were changing as gender, colour and creed found the capacity to demand their rights and place as equals.

Humanity was beginning to realise and understand its capacity and true worth and to lead us to the place where we exist now.

In this modern world, made even smaller by the expanding field of technology, Spirit have chosen to enable us work through what they knew to be the means to an end. It is no longer necessary for a single individual to be upheld as the ideal medium or communicator of divine love and spiritual understanding. This gift is now open to us all and we can all be responsible for encouraging others to stand up and recognise the wonderful truth of our true spiritual nature. They did this, and continue to do so, by offering proof of an everlasting spirit through communication and recognition from one individual to another.

Providing Proof

It was in the early twentieth century, amidst an era of personal growth and expansion that Spirit worked their very hardest to draw society in to the truth of spirit contact in a bid to show to the world that this was not just a superstition or system of uneducated beliefs, but a possible empirical and evidential process. Persons of note from all backgrounds and levels of education found themselves able to embrace, identify and more importantly challenge and prove the evidence, information and phenomena that came to light.

To this end there was a great deal of recorded physical evidence of spirit contact and mediumistic ability, from Spirit paintings to rapping and movement of objects, recorded within the early days and development of Mediumship as we know it today. Spirit intended this, as we were still requiring not only just proof, but also proof beyond all reasonable doubt. This was readily given, purely in a bid to shift the perceptions of all who were to witness such events and to permit clarity and openness to all the incredible physical manifestations made possible through our Spiritual connection.

Slowly the more educated and sceptical began to take notice, particularly noted men of science such as Dr A Russel Walker, the co-discoverer with Charles Darwin of the Theory of Evolution, and Sir William Crookes. Both men spent a who spent a great deal of time investigating with intent to perhaps debunk and prove fraud the evidence brought forward during spiritualist séances before finally promoting that what was being recorded and seen across the world was indeed a phenomena that could be proven. Not only proven to the believers, but in ways and methods that gave credence to what they saw just as readily as any other science. They witnessed events that made them not only believers, but also great advocates of the existence of Spiritual contact. The interest of such learned and educated men encouraged others to stand up and take note of what was developing before their eyes, that they were witnessing the development of human awareness of the realm of spirit, and the growing truth that existence beyond the end of our physical life is not merely a possibility, but an actuality.

In the mid to latter half of the nineteenth century, growth and development of Spiritualist groups had become so widespread that many thought it to be desirable to unite under a common banner and a National Federation of Spiritualists was born. From this Federation rose many great pioneers of the Spiritualist movement, it truly seemed as though the world of spirit had finally found it footing in the message that was being delivered.

With the foundation of a dedicated movement, Spiritualism began to grow and expand within the public consciousness, yet despite this the movement had a long way to go before public, and religious, acceptance would become commonplace.

The Modern World

As the nineteenth century waned and the new twentieth century came around time there were many who dedicated themselves to the expansion and education of the world of spirit. As the first Lyceums opened around the world, Alfred Kitson became a devotee of the importance of the teaching of the younger members of society the truth of spirit contact and eventually developed the Lyceum Manual, taking development and education of spirit into new fields and areas of specialisation and paving the way for the next generation of spiritualists to begin their first tentative steps on the route to truth.

All through the early twentieth century, spiritualist expansion increased and attracted all comers to attend and make up their minds on the evidence brought forward during both private séances and church meetings. As spiritualism grew so too did the evidence, drawing forward messages of love, hope, and guidance from many in spirit such as Silver Birch via the medium Maurice Barbanell, and evidential physical manifestation and spirit writing from gifted mediums such as Reverend George Vale Owen.

Many incredible mediums took their skills out into the world, often to their detriment and sometimes punishment. Many were faced with prison terms and sentences under the Witchcraft Act such as the famous Glasgow medium Helen Duncan who was were imprisoned for her remarkable Mediumship and her beliefs. To think that this was in 1944 and not under the auspices of a less enlightened time is truly remarkable.

At this time, the eyes of the scientific community focused heavily on the spiritualist belief and the foundations of many modern psychic science methodologies were formed through the efforts of noted members of the scientific community such as Sir Oliver Lodge and Dr William J Crawford.

Toward the end of the Twentieth Century, many great mediums began to write and leave behind legacies for the future in books, notes and sometimes through acts of dedicated generosity. Through the efforts of many selfless individuals such as Harry Edwards, Gordon Higgenson, and J Arthur Findlay, the knowledge and experience of the past has been immortalised for the generations to come. Perhaps it was indeed Spirit viewing the world and age ahead that advised and drove so many to produce and save fine bodies of work and to give so much of themselves that future generations may learn from those who were better placed to lay the groundwork for us all.

Today, through the efforts of so many of those mentioned here and, many more not mentioned, the practice of Spiritualism is now widely accepted as a modern science, philosophy and religion. This transition was not a smooth one and timing was important in order to escape the pitfalls and trials of superstitious belief and prejudice. The latter twentieth century saw the world go through many changes as wars were waged and power struggles encompassed the globe yet in the midst of all this, through the dedicated efforts and sacrifice of many, Spiritualism was finally received and acknowledged for the science, philosophy and religion that it truly is.

Fortunately, today, we live in a more open-minded and less closed civilisation, or at least we pretend to. Within our society the role of the medium today is undergoing yet another huge paradigm shift in the public consciousness yet although the level of awareness has changed, has the viewpoint of the public been altered to be more positive or negative.

For many the public jury is still out on the validity and quality of each and every one who proclaims to be able to link with the Spirit of our loved ones. This is understandable, for it has taken thousands of years of spiritual understanding to reach even this point and in that time Spirit has tried so very hard to get their message through. Yet almost every time it has been deflected, blocked or even distorted along the way, Why is this so? Primarily because the ego inside all of us only wants for itself, and the possibility that a truth of continued life out-with this physical existence can be an often terrifying option to behold.

If the purpose of this life is to learn and grow from all experience, then the ego nature to defend and protect becomes diminished within the scope of our lives every time that we are able to take another step forward. We need not truly fear any of these life experiences when we know that they are ultimately put forward to challenge us and to act as a lesson to be learned, and not obstacles to our very continued existence.

The pace and way of life between the past and the world today has changed dramatically, even in the last twenty years we have travelled further along the technological route than we did in the previous one hundred years and there appears to be no stopping the progress and momentum of human endeavour and accomplishment. Is it possible that along the way we have forgotten the message in light of the methods? Modern technology has brought spirituality into a new light and any channel on any network can at any time be showing a cacophony of television shows, movies and presentation of Mediumship, Psychism and the world of the Paranormal as a means of entertainment. Access to the world of Spirit has been simplified and glorified, but has it been brought to us in a true light and what is to become of the public perception of the message and the truth of our perpetual soul? What direction, understanding and message are we truly giving out and where does the role of the medium fit into society today?

Mediaship vs. Mediumship

The role and purpose of the medium today, and especially within the last fifteen years, has changed radically within the public perception.

While the rising upsurge in public interest in the paranormal, the strange and the unusual has served as an unexpected platform for greater awareness of the spirit world, this has proven to be a double edged sword. Although this increases the public perception of the possibility that there is more to our existence in this life than simply a physical expression and state of being, it also fails to accurately capture the reasons for our increased expansion of consciousness and the greater awareness of the spirit within.

Does this actually assist and aid in the progress and spread of Mediumship and knowledge of Spirit Contact to a greater audience, or does this instead present a false front as to the true nature and miracle that we see in every contact. More importantly, is the message that we should be delivering, actually being delivered? How much does the public understand about the importance of not only the messages within the contact, but that the actual contact and communication is even possible at all? What, in fact, do they get from their own experience of spirit contact?

Paranormal Misconceptions

The rising popularity of paranormal television shows, portraying mediums as human 'spirit detectors' has massively changed the public perception of the medium. But is the medium now very often on the verge of being looked upon as merely another form of late night entertainment? Is it possible that this greater coverage, and very subtle editing on many of these shows, is putting Mediumship into a position that could very well do more damage than good? What will happen if we continue to allow the gift of communication with our loved ones to become such a trivial focus and perceived notion for entertainment purposes only?

For many, the medium has become nothing more than another entertainer, a potential stage show, and a means of passing time on a night out with friends. For every church service, there are as many if not more 'Psychic Nights' that bring in four, five or six times the amount of viewers and audience. Some come along to see the show, others come along to support their friends, and in amidst all of this there are the few who desperately need to receive words of comfort, often without even realising the truth of this.

It is often unfortunate that this is the only chance some of these people will get to once again re-unite with their loved ones. Perhaps they would be too embarrassed to attend a Spiritualist Church, or perhaps their families and friends would frown or make fun of them. There may be many reasons, but the event and the night will rarely ever touch them in the way it should unless the focus and the intent behind everyone involved remains true to our own Spirit within and the source of divine love.

Having attended a few of these events myself, I have seen

and heard many worrying factors from the members of the audience both during and after the event that hints of a lack of understanding or even desire to see the wonder of what Spirit is trying to teach us. Reactions from people such as derision or anger being aimed at mediums, to snide comments and a definite lack of participation and desire to be part of the communication, even down to outright disbelief and talk of the Spirit communication being 'evil', I have witnessed them all being levied at mediums and spirit workers first-hand.

The demand for mediums to be just as they are seen on television and in the media, providing unbelievably accurate information with every contact and connection made, lies at the forefront of many who attend.

Everyone wants to see what they witness on the television or on the internet. Yet most are often unaware that many of the shows and programmes they see are distilled and edited version of a much longer event. They fail to see the full picture being presented and very often miss out on the meaning and purpose behind the contact. All many want is to be entertained and more and more the medium is being manoeuvred into a position whereby, if they fail to jump through the necessary hoops and tick the requisite boxes, then they are either no good or simply less than adequate.

Losing the Message

Evidence of events, survival of personality, and communication with Spirit is no longer enough for many. The evidence must be more accurate, the communication must be longer, have more information, be more unerringly accurate and precise in every shape and sense of the word, otherwise it is no good.

Ironically, even when all this is done and delivered just as demanded, there are many who label the medium as either fake or as setting up the whole things. Either way, the medium cannot win. They are either labelled as 'fake' for being too good, or sometimes just 'bad' for being inaccurate.

Where has the original message gone?

Despite all this, there is still a rising demand and passion for displays of Mediumship. Every week in any town in the United Kingdom you may find a poster or flyer in newspapers or shop windows indicating a psychic evening or demonstration of Mediumship. Online social networks are ablaze with invites and notifications of so many events that it is literally not possible to attend them all. Clearly there is a public demand for Mediumship or Psychism, and people will pay to attend by the droves.

Most of these events will be comfortably booked well in advance. Clearly there is a demand for them, but what are the motives for attendance? Is it to witness Spirit, or is it merely a night out of the house and away from the family.

We must always remember that Mediumship, and Spirit Communication, is not a form of entertainment and has never been. In the past Public demonstrations given by many of the spiritual pioneers of the Spiritualist Movement sought to teach and learn and offer the opportunity for the public to see and witness the miraculous communication and links to Spirit that can be attained. The purpose then was to educate and to open the minds of the public to the truth of Spiritual Contact for healing of our grief and loss, and for the betterment of humanity and Spirit itself. Can we truly say that this is the case today?

Responsible Mediumship

It is important that we remember the personal nature of each and every individual journey through this life. Many who experience the communication from spirit are not yet ready to accept this and so push back against the possibility equally. This may simply be where they are in life at this time. Perhaps the loss and grief is too raw or too fresh to endure once again. Either way, we should always be ready to step away if need be.

As mediums, we have a responsibility to ensure that the gift of Spirit communication, healing and the positive power of our Spiritual nature is protected at all times. This also includes knowing when and where to use our abilities and skills in an appropriate fashion and for the best and purest of intentions. Our role as a worker for Spirit, and the healing that we do, should never be forgotten and should always be at the forefront of any work that we become involved in.

Unless we begin to once again realise this and learn from the lessons and prejudices of the past, we may once again be opening ourselves, and the Spirit world, up to attack and ridicule. It is not merely enough to want to spread the knowledge and guidance from Spirit.

The place and timing to do so, like that undertaken by all those who have gone before us to promote Spiritualism worldwide, is of such vital importance.

A few years ago I made a personal choice regarding my own development and pathway for the future of my Mediumship. I now choose to turn my hand to serving spiritualist churches or groups, working with private individuals and those who truly want to experience the wonder of spirit communication and contact with the Spirit world. I gladly give my time to and work with events where there is a goal and binding force to improve and aid others and promote the positive, genuine, and healing aspects of Spirit contact. I choose to do so not only to protect myself, but also out of respect for the communicators both here and in Spirit.

As I stated before, my only exception to this rule is where the work is being done for Charity, for I find that in these instances we are able rise up above the more selfless purpose within the energy and soul of everyone who attends. I often find that Spirit are happier and more ready to come through at such times too. They prefer it when we are all united and work together for a common cause, particularly if that cause is founded in aiding each other in some way.

We all have our own preferences on how and when to work and to get the very best from ourselves we must always be listened to that Spirit within. It will know what you need in order to progress. However, we truly get the very best from our work when we are in accord with the flow of Spiritual energy that surrounds us at all times.

We should never work from a place or point of negativity or which acts against our own nature, instead always choose to work from the light within and for the betterment of both yourself and others. Spirit and everyone else will always get the best from you when you do so.

Confusing the Paranormal

As mentioned earlier, there has been a massive rise in the popularity and public demand for not just Mediumship, but also the paranormal. Often the two are considered to be linked but the truth is that there is nothing at all paranormal about Mediumship and the work that is undertaken for Spirit and the spirit realm.

We are Spirit, not just beings that link to it and each and every one of us has at some time or another been a part of that Spirit realm. In choosing to come here we make a choice to do so in order to learn and grow. You rally cannot emphasise this enough. When we link into and work with Spirit and Spirit contact, it is no different to picking up a phone and talking to a loved one, or them paying you a visit. It is one of the most natural things that we can be part of, to be close to the Spirit of another.

The term 'paranormal' means something that is above or beyond the normal. The actual act of reaching out to and communicating with the Spirit of our loved ones is in fact no different to speaking to any other person within this physical life. This is something that we do each and every day of our lives and we think nothing of it. What then is so hard to accept that we continue to do so? What aspect of our human nature is it that seeks to label our Spiritual self as something that is to be doubted?

When we see a friend or acquaintance in need, we want to reach out and help. If we need to speak and clear up an issue we will do what we can to meet with the persons involved and raise it. When we feel hurt or a desire to be healed, we will seek out those best suited to assist us. We do all this in our everyday life and think little of it. It is exactly the same with our Spiritual and eternal existence as well. Although our form and substance may no longer be tied to the physical realm, we are still aware of this life and those within it. If you could, would you not also want to reach out and do what you can for those you care about. Is this truly a state this is above the normal condition for your Spirit and soul in this existence?

The concept and evidence of Mediumship and Spirit contact may appear to be unbelievable and out of the frame of reference for most of us, however it is truly not so. Every day of our life in this physical plane we are surrounded by our friends and loved ones in Spirit and they readily make themselves known to us at every opportunity. Like everything else in life, if we are not open to the possibility and the opportunity, the moment will simply pass us by. This is particularly true if we cloud our minds to all the potential options available by focusing only on specific aspects of our life, and our understanding of all that is within it.

Keeping it all on the ground

It is natural for all of us to be curious, inquisitive and to have an innate desire and drive to investigate and to learn to unravel the mysteries presented to us. Not only is there great prestige to be gained from the pursuit and understanding of new methodologies and discoveries in this incredible experience of life that we are part of, but it also brings a greater level of understanding and often improved quality of life to everyone whom this knowledge touches.

Nothing that we truly are told should ever be taken on board fully without first arriving at our own conclusions based on experience and participation. This is particularly true for those who wish to follow a Spiritual path. Everything that we see and experience should be questioned honestly, not with intent to disprove, but with intent to participate and to reach a greater level of understanding with which to expand our own awareness and consciousness. The greatest challenge is to do so without allowing the ego to take control and to over-ride the capacity of our human minds to accept the possibilities that lie around us.

In light of the ghost hunting and paranormal boom it becomes very easy to misinterpret Spirit contact as evidence of paranormal events and happenings, particularly with the correct lighting, sound effects and reactions that we see within the modern media.

Yet, we forget that many of these televised shows are intentionally produced and structured in order to appeal to a viewing public with an interest. That interest may be in evidence, in events, in debunking, or in causing a thrill and moment of chill akin to telling ghost stories around the camp fire. Either way it is being targeted specifically for that purpose.

I am, like many others, personally fond of these forms of entertainment and always have been, but I choose to accept them for what they are. Anything on television is provided for entertainment, and these are no different than an action movie or a chat show as far as I am concerned. It is merely entertainment targeted to a specific paranormal interest group and bears little or no relevance to genuine spiritual communication and contact. Taken in the correct context it is all good fun, however we are led to believe that most of this is real. Cue atmospheric music, sinister voiceovers and stand-in actors and you have the full package. The danger lies in the fact that many fail to see the difference between this and the events and circumstances that occur in the real world. Many of these shows are designed to cause fear, it is good for ratings, appeals to our natural primal terrors and gives us the chills just like ghost stories around the camp fire. This is not to be confused with Spirituality, Spiritualism or mediumship in any way, for that power exists in the light and in the soul and Spirit within us all and has no bearing upon what we see in the supposed 'paranormal' world and media. It is vital that we learn to separate the two entirely.

Spirit do no harm

Spirit have no need to cause fear or discomfort, it serves no purpose to them and does very little to promote understanding or awareness of the spirit realm. It actually would do quite the opposite and they are all so very aware of that.

Yes, it is true that Spirit may be able to reach into our lives and to affect or manipulate our world to a minor degree. Whenever they do so, however, it would never be to cause harm or hurt but would be intended to guide or comfort. Never forget that these are our loved ones who come to us; devoid of all the lifelong baggage they accrued and returned to their true spiritual self. Why would they try to harm or cause fear, it simply does not happen.

On the odd occasion that Spirit do make something occur that we consider to be fearful it is generally the human part of our own mind that picks up on this and which applies the fear to the event.

We are all highly charged and emotional beings, every day we undergo numerous chemical changes and alterations that affect not only our body chemistry, but also how we react to the world around us. When we see events that upset of cause discomfort, they are all stored away for future reference. All that we see and experience is packaged, stored and shelved within the chemical mix of our intellectual and emotional responses for that time when the reference may need to be brought out and dusted down for use.

When you add in to this our capacity for imagination and creativity, it is easy to see how and why we are often fearful of not only what we think we experience, but also what we apply to that experience from within ourselves.

It is always important that all of us on our spiritual journey be aware of the need to remain firmly grounded in all the work that we do.

Humans fear, Spirit does not

I have been approached so many times by people who see the paranormal in everyday events and look for guidance on the subject. Most of the time, many or all of the phenomena they experience is purely manifestation of their own fears, insecurities and worries given shape and form. This occurs through their own manipulation of their individual psychic capability, usually driven by stress, fear and all other negative emotions. All it takes is for them to tap into the background energy that exists around us and then events occur. As soon as they acknowledge the actual problems they face, the phenomena stops.

At other times it is our loved ones in Spirit coming close, often making themselves known to us either in remembrance or in offering comfort. It is easy for us to allow our fears and insecurities to deny the actual love and contact we feel, and for the ego self to overlap this with many of the fears and superstitions that we have locked away over the years. In releasing our fear, we are ourselves released from our doubt.

This is in part, one of the lessons that we still have to learn and work upon in this life. In learning to understand our Spirit within and then be aware of our true Spiritual nature to heal, we can remove the fears associated with so much of the miraculous communication and links to spirit that happen each and every day.

We do not need to imagine what it would be like to once again hold in our arms, or to touch and experience the closeness of a loved one. All those who have passed beyond this physical life are more than aware of our thoughts and rejoice when we acknowledge their presence and invite them here to join us. It does not need to be a complex or demanding ritual that we undertake in order to achieve this. Often it is as easy as sitting quietly and allowing our body and mind to just stop being so caught up in the physical world. In these moments, if we let them happen, we can relax and open our senses to everything around us without distraction.

Put aside all your doubts and thoughts of discouragement. Do not fear what others may think or feel and be free from all that may hold you back or seek to put doubt in your mind. You are safe and whole and you are a spiritual being in your own right.

Imagine for a moment the joy you may be able to experience

at requesting a gentle touch or holding of your hand, or detecting the lightest waft of a favourite scent worn by someone we hold dear in our hearts. When you do this, you begin to understand the wondrous and beautiful gift that we all have to expand our spiritual self and find our way back home to those who love us, and never leave us. We learn to open our eyes for the first time in our lives.

With clear vision and all doubts cast aside, your true nature and spiritual self is permitted to shine and shows the way forward and our methods to progress in our spiritual journey becomes clear.

Chapter 12

Positive Action for Progress

The Future of Spirituality

EVERY DAY WE DIG deeper into the mysteries of not only the world around us, but the universe and beyond. Every stone unturned draws us into to deeper questions regarding our place in this universe, and what we are to do with all the knowledge and answers that we uncover.

We all have a role to play in understanding and carefully unwrapping of the greater picture and grand fabric that forms the tapestry of this universe. Regardless of our own personal beliefs or direction, each and every one of us is wound up within this pattern, and we all have our part to play. For some it will be the scientist applying empirical values to define the physical limitations and boundaries to which we need to apply pressure to move. For others it will be the role of the Spiritualist, seeking ways and means to better understand the meaning of the systems in play beyond the merely mundane and physical, to bridge the gap between the Spirit within and the life in which it learns. All are of equal importance and all have chosen to live through that particular experience.

Our journey, though, remains the same for all. The quest as laid out before us is to once again find and realise that spiritual part of ourselves that is locked into this existence. To rediscover the Spirit and soul intrinsically linked to the divine source of love and healing that is around us at all times.

Every discovery changes the world and our understanding of it in one small way or another and sends ripples of amendment through the very fabric and tapestry of life itself. Often the smallest of things can affect the greatest of changes given enough power behind it and the time and space to develop.

Within this constantly changing environment and highly technological world, it can be all too easy for us to forget the power that we hold in favour of merely qualifying the simple, physical aspects of life. When we think of power and change, we tend to do so only in terms of affecting permanence on this world and in this time. We often do not consider the change and alteration of our Spiritual self and the capacity for it to affect these changes as part of an eternal existence. We do, sometimes, lose track of our spiritual potential when we progress through this physical life.

Yet we can never truly forget every aspect our spiritual self and the true light of love and understanding that has the capacity to shine forth. We may misplace or lose touch with it from time to time but all it takes is the smallest of actions and the time necessary to instigate the wind of change in any given situation.

The future of Spiritual growth for world lies in the hands of all of us and not merely the next generation. Any single individual has the potential to place a seed of growth whenever they find themselves on the quest for their own understanding and truth. All the people and lives that we touch, we change in one way or another, and this moves out in a wave of Spiritual echoes across the face of the world around us.

It is so vitally important that we be aware of the power that we have. We all hold great potential within us for all of our words and actions to affect the environment around us. As we all become more spiritually attuned and spiritually aware, so also do we achieve a greater balance and understanding of the spiritual self within.

As we move on into the future and we grow and learn and become one with our Spirit within, we make small changes in the capability for the Spirit realm to come to us and so we begin to close that gap that has separated us. We must keep our intentions linked to the true and loving emanations that echo from the Spirit realm, for these will guide us toward actions not just for the benefit of ourselves but also the future of mankind to direct it in ways that it needs to travel forward, and to grow positively.

It is easy to disassociate oneself from the world when we see the traumas and horrors that humanity is capable of inflicting upon itself and its fellows. The greater the push toward the physical existence and the problems and trials of this physical life, the greater the challenge we face to recognise the Spirit within. It becomes so easy to close the doors of the mind to the world and to seek solace in the immediate environment only and be caught up in oneself. Yet we often do not, and it is in the most dire and difficult of times that we truly come together as a single, unified and Spiritual humanity.

As a single humanity following a singular purpose, we can rise above and become so much more than a gathering of independent members only interested in their own survival. It is in the aftermath of the worst of times that we see the very best that each and every one of us has to offer. Our soul and spirit can truly empathise with the suffering of others and our compassion for our fellow Spirit comes to the fore. We realise that no-one need to suffer in silence and that together we can be capable of such positive direction and growth.

Truly, as the world changes in so many positive and negative ways, there is greater need than ever for any and all who are able to open up to and realise their Spirit within. Each of us has the potential to be not only an advocate but an ambassador for the Spirit realm and all that the realisation of our true spiritual potential has to offer.

Every discovery brings with it new questions and even greater challenges and there will never come a time when we are not presented with these. What will change in time is our familiarity and closeness to the Spirit within and the manner in which we deal with these opportunities to continue to grow. This is why we must protect not only our history of spiritual development, but why we must continue to pave the way forward for all who follow.

We need not be perfect throughout our life, but we should at least make sure that all our predecessors remain inspired throughout their time as they follow on behind us. In taking steps forward we preserve this continuous quest for the cycle of growth, of life, and of undying and everlasting love that burns at the core of each and every soul.

This will start when you wish it to and when you believe that you are worthy of this journey, for Spirit will be waiting for your acknowledge and will do all they can to assist once you begin to accept your potential.

Be Inspired, Be Inspiring

History does have a tendency to repeat itself and we all have the opportunity to learn from the past from so many great and wonderful teachers. In choosing to enter into this spiritual journey and in finding the courage to progress we must also be prepared to step into the footsteps of these individuals and to continue the journey from the point it was left behind.

We are all often intrigued by the events that we read or hear of from our past. While it is good to compare and seek inspiration from this, we should never become so locked in the past that we lost sight of the present. How can we hope to influence the future if we are not yet engaging with the world around us?

Remember, we are all pioneers of our faith and belief. We cannot hope to be in any way compared to those from the past, for that was their time and their place, and their moment to affect change. Had they all being looking to their own past then the spiritual understanding and awareness that we have today would not exist. Fortunately many of these individuals had the presence and self-belief to trust in the truth of the Spirit world and the impact that this would have on the world of our time and beyond. These individuals did not work for themselves, like all good pioneers, they worked so hard and so tirelessly so that we may have what is in place around us today. They worked tirelessly for us.

The future of Spiritualism and spirituality needs tireless, responsible and grounded people who wish to take their knowledge, understanding, and the love from Spirit away from this moment and into the future. Not for us, but for the many generations and Spiritual souls to learn from and to experience the miracle of connection to the Spirit realm.

We are entering a new age of awareness and understanding. Many are throwing off the hitherto accepted boundaries of society and the limits imposed upon them by their physical existence. Every new generation is possessing so much more capacity for understanding and openness of the Spirit within, due to the small ripples and echoes that we have all been creating for so, so long.

More and more people are opening up to the possibilities of spiritual contact and the gift to our lives on the knowledge of eternal capacity for growth, learning and love for another. Spirit are overjoyed to see us realise and progress within every aspect of our growth and want nothing more from each of us than to carry this legacy of hope and truth into the future. You are already doing it now, simply by reading this. Your thoughts are affecting change, not just in yourself, but also in the world and all around and within you. You are already giving more hope to the future simply because of that resonating and positive Spirit within.

We work best when in that place and time where all of our facets are permitted to align and function to the maximum of their ability. When this occurs the universe and everything within it comes into focus and all of life seems to flow. Remember that you are in effect a whole and perfect being, that you spiritual light is the true and everlasting part of you that will continue to shine well beyond the limits of this temporary existence.

The future is as much your responsibility and your inheritance as it is also your legacy.

The future is all of ours to make.

All it takes is that positive thought.

To Trust in Sprit.

To Trust in you.

About the Author

STEVEN WK SCOTT IS a working Medium and a member of the Spiritualist National Union. He lives in Ayrshire, Scotland with his wife Mhairi, his Stepdaughter, and a myriad of animals. This is his first non-fiction work.